Presented To:

_____

From:

_____

Date:

_____

# BATTLE for the MIND

BOOKS BY NOEL JONES

*Battle for the Mind*

*God's Gonna Make You Laugh*

*Vow of Prosperity*

AVAILABLE FROM DESTINY IMAGE PUBLISHERS

# BATTLE for the MIND

## How You **CAN** Think the Thoughts of God

# Noel Jones

*and*

# Dr. Georgianna Land

EXPANDED EDITION

DESTINY IMAGE. PUBLISHERS, INC.

P.O. Box 310, Shippensburg, PA 17257-0310

*"Promoting Inspired Lives."*

This book and all other Destiny Image, Revival Press, MercyPlace, Fresh Bread, Destiny Image Fiction, and Treasure House books are available at Christian bookstores and distributors worldwide.

For a U.S. bookstore nearest you, call 1-800-722-6774.

For more information on foreign distributors, call 717-532-3040.

Reach us on the Internet: www.destinyimage.com.

ISBN 13 TP: 978-0-7684-4140-6

ISBN 13 Ebook: 978-0-7684-8821-0

For Worldwide Distribution, Printed in the U.S.A.

2 3 4 5 6 7 8 / 16 15 14 13 12

# DEDICATION

To my son, Noel, and his wife, Dr. Cozzette; my son, Eric, and his wife, Angel; and my daughter, Tifani.

To my precious grandchildren, Lena and Ian.

Also, to my father and mother, Bishop Robert W. and Marjorie N. Jones.

# ACKNOWLEDGMENTS

Dr. Land and I wish to express heartfelt thanks to Don Milam at Destiny Image Publishers for his encouragement and partnership on this project from the very beginning. Don has given us helpful feedback and suggestions that were critical to bringing this manuscript to publication; and without his kindness, understanding, and patience, it would have been impossible. Thank you, Don.

We also extend our sincere thanks to Rhonda Hamilton for editing the manuscript. Rhonda, you have helped us so much, and we appreciate your constant care and understanding as you have given so much of your time reading and rereading many pages.

# CONTENTS

# FOREWORD

I live in Los Angeles, California, but for five years, I worked in Washington, D.C. as host of a nightly television talk show on Black Entertainment Television (BET). During that five-year period, every Monday morning I would catch American Airlines flight #77 to Washington Dulles, arriving just in time for my live show; and almost every Friday morning, I would catch American Airlines flight #144 back to Los Angeles.

Countless times during that five-year period, I was asked why I didn't just move to D.C., why I returned to Los Angeles every weekend, racking up millions of frequent flier miles. My answer was always the same. In a word—well, two actually—*Noel Jones*. Bishop Noel Jones is, in my estimation, without equal on the circuit of today's prophetic witnesses. Then again, I suspect that's exactly what most parishioners think about their pastor. But here's what makes me right—most of the other powerful and prophetic preachers will second my motion. Jones has style and substance. They know it, and many try to emulate it. Following are two funny stories to prove my point.

I heard a preacher in Dallas tell of how he always wanted to work the mic(rophone) like Jones does when he's getting his "hoop" on. He moves the mic back and forth in a quick motion while he leans back and simultaneously puts his hand behind his ear while the organist follows him as he changes key, "hooping" up the scale. And the audience is gone—completely gone. Now that...that's style. Except when this preacher in Dallas tried it, he busted himself in the mouth with the mic, blood gushed everywhere! While Jones was pleading the Blood, the other guy was bleeding the blood! Style.

But what's style without substance? Not much more than sounding brass and tinkling cymbal.

The substance of Jones's messages is already *legendary*—and I don't use that word lightly.

Consider this.

Jones arrived in a city in Texas to preach a three-day revival. The pastor of the local church picked up Jones at the airport, and during the ride to the church, he casually asked Bishop Jones what he intended to preach that night. Jones told him. The pastor encouraged Jones to preach something else because he had just preached that same subject a few Sundays prior! Jones suggested another sermon. "Nope. Already did that, too," the preacher responded. Turns out that this preacher (like many others) had listened to Jones's tapes and, shall we say, "repurposed" them.

His substance is so substantial, his hermeneutics so tight, his insight so keen, and his observations so interestingly unusual that young preachers everywhere want to be like him. Down to the suits and matching handkerchiefs. What a compliment. They say that imitation is the greatest form of flattery. But there's only one "First Noel," if you know what I mean. Often imitated, but never duplicated.

Because of his leadership, our church, the City of Refuge, was about to become the City of *Refuse*. That is to say, unless we built something quick, we were going to continue having to turn folks away. Nowhere to park. Nowhere to sit. Nowhere to stand. And that's no way to treat folks trying to find a little Heaven after catching hell all week long.

So Jones says to me, "Ahh, Tavis, we have a problem."

I said, "Yes, and it's all your fault." He smiled. But what a great problem to have—being one of the fastest-growing churches in America—which leads to my final thought.

At the moment, Jones is still the best-kept secret in the Church. But not for long. More books, more television, more exposure. Don't be the last to discover the preacher's preacher—Noel Jones. Hear him, see him, read him, enjoy him, and then pass him on—for the Kingdom.

I feel sorry for folks like that young preacher in Texas who "repurposed" Jones's text. In just a little while, it's going to be hard, really hard, to do that and not get caught.

Keep the faith!

—TAVIS SMILEY
Author and National TV and Radio Commentator
Founder, Tavis Smiley Foundation

# SECTION ONE

# BECOMING A SPIRITUAL PERSON

The postmodern world is an eclectic mishmash of varying philosophies and approaches to life. The transition from the modern world to the post-modern world was initiated back in the '60s. While the Cinderella Church was sleeping, the world was changing. Truths that were embedded into the fabric of the American culture were under attack. Patriotism, moral-ity, community, theology, and the culture were under attack. The hippie movement was at the forefront of this attack, while science joined in the frontal assault. The Church did not understand the nature of this change and reacted with judgment and condemnation.

The hippies of the '60s were gradually assimilated back into the culture and moved from protest to sanction. They became corporate America. They drifted from communal living to suburban life. They lost their souls and went back into the box. In the postmodern world, there is no anchor, no foundation. Men and women are looking for reality. Drugs didn't work and neither does the dollar. The world is looking for its soul.

In this section, we will explore the internal conflict that comes when a soul is detached from its Maker. The soul has to get out of the box and find its original self. It is a journey that will take the spiritual traveler to an inward space—the mind. It is in the mind where the journey begins. It is the last frontier, and if we can conquer the mind, we can find our uniqueness and begin to express our original selves without the restraint of preconceived opinions and judgments. This is the journey toward true spirituality.

# THE STREET THAT LEADS TO SUCCESS—TRUTH FROM THE BOOK OF ROMANS

In A.D. 386, a 32-year-old North African intellectual, now living in Milan, Italy, was sitting in the garden of one of his friends, overwhelmed with grief and sorrow. This man was one of the great scholars of his day, but he was in a battle with his mind, seeking the meaning of life as he also struggled with lust and immorality. His mother, Monica, whom he loved deeply, was distressed with the fact that her young son was living with a mistress. Great sorrow had a grip on his heart as he realized that he had no power to break the hold of immorality on his life.

Sitting there in the garden, his attention was aroused by the voice of a young man whose words rang in his ears, "Pick up and read! Pick up and read!" At the same time, he noticed next to him a scroll that his friend had been reading. As he picked it up and began to read, it appeared as though the words of the apostle Paul to the Romans (13:13-14) leaped off the page: *"...not in revelry and drunkenness, not in lewdness and lust, not in strife and envy. But put on the Lord Jesus Christ, and make no provision for the flesh, to fulfill its lusts."* It was at that moment that a spiritual power descended upon him, and a faith was born within him.

In his autobiography, *Confessions*, he wrote these poignant words to describe what happened that day:

> I neither wished nor needed to read further. At once, with the
> last words of this sentence, it was as if a light of relief from all

anxiety flooded into my heart. All the shadows of doubt were dispelled.[1]

The name of this young academic scholar was Aurelius Augustine. Augustine would go on to become the Bishop of Hippo in North Africa, a great pastor, and a Christian theologian. His writings would shape the course of Christian theology to this day.

## A Monk Encounters the Apostle Paul

In August 1513, an Augustinian monk who was a Professor of Bible in the University of Wittenberg, Germany, was troubled with his spiritual life. For years he had been trying to find peace with God, yet all his religious efforts could not bring the peace and joy that he was seeking. He had no confidence that God accepted him, no matter how hard he tried to please Him. Troubled by his lack of spiritual clarity, he opened the Book of Romans and was reading chapter 1, verse 17, "...*The righteousness of God is revealed...by faith...*" (NIV). This young monk could not comprehend what Paul was talking about because his mind had been telling him that God's righteousness judged him rather than saved him. In an effort to penetrate the meaning of Paul's words, he wrote:

> I greatly longed to understand Paul's letter to the Romans, and nothing stood in the way but that one expression, "the righteousness of God," because I took it to mean that righteousness whereby God is righteous and acts righteously in punishing the unrighteous.... Night and day I pondered until...I grasped the truth that the righteousness of God is that righteousness whereby, through grace and sheer mercy, he justifies us by faith. Thereupon I felt myself to be reborn and to have gone through open doors into paradise. The whole of Scripture took on a new meaning, and whereas before "the righteousness of God" had filled me with hate, now it became to me inexpressibly sweet in greater love. This message of Paul became to me a gateway into heaven.[2]

I am quite sure you know this monk. His name is Martin Luther. The discovery that he made that day not only changed his life, but would lead to the greatest reformation in the history of the Church. When Martin Luther nailed his 95 theses to the Wittenburg door, he launched revival fires that spread across 16th-century Europe.

## AN ANGLICAN'S ENCOUNTER WITH THE BOOK OF ROMANS

In the evening of May 24, 1738, a young Anglican minister ventured out to attend a meeting with some Moravians who were gathering at Barclays Bank on Aldersgate Street in London. This young man had started his religious career with such high expectations. He had graduated from Oxford, where he had been a member of a radical group of Christians called the "Holy Club," a club started by his younger brother. From there he crossed the ocean to work with the Indians in the state of Georgia. He then returned to England in despair and disillusionment because of his lack of spiritual power. As the troubled young man walked into the meeting that night, the most notable event in 18th-century English history was only seconds away. As he was sitting there in the meeting, someone began to read from Luther's Preface to the Book of Romans, where he describes what happens when people open their hearts in simple faith toward the living God.

That young man was John Wesley. In his own style, the young minister wrote these classic words:

> I felt my heart strangely warmed. I felt I did trust in Christ,
> Christ alone for salvation, and an assurance was given me that
> He had taken away my sins, even mine, and saved me from the
> law of sin and death.[3]

The warmth that was generated in his heart that night was about to set all England ablaze with glorious revival.

At the age of 35, his life was changed, and there would be no going back to the old ways of religion. The direction for his life was now set on a new path—one that would focus on this message of faith in Christ. He would know for the rest of his life that the God who is reflected in the face of Jesus Christ had come down to earth to visit him and had done for Wesley precisely what he could never have done for himself. His earlier zeal for holy living would remain with him, but it would be enhanced with an intense thankfulness for the grace and mercy given to him—a grace and mercy that was not based upon any work that he had ever done, but on Christ's work alone.

## THE ALTAR WITHIN YOU

The mind is the seat of all spiritual and carnal conflict. I'm sure that you've noticed by now that the act of becoming a Christian has introduced many internal conflicts into your life. Conversely, one doesn't really come to know God until he or she experiences personal conflict. Somebody might have, mistakenly, assured you that when you come to God, your troubles will be over. Well, somebody was lying. I'm sure you have learned by now, as many people have, that walking with God is not conflict-free. Whenever people respond to the internal motivation of the Word and come to God, while at the same time cease to react to the external stimulus of the world, they will encounter resistance and turmoil. In fact, the process of moving from the external (depending on a lot of outside sources) to the internal (depending on God and self) can be chaotic at best. Paul, in the Book of Romans, addresses this conflict as he endeavors to define and clarify the opposing forces that operate to gain influence on the mind. When we come to Romans chapter 7, we find that he laments his own condition:

> But now, it is no longer I who do it, but sin that dwells in me. For I know that in me (that is, in my flesh) nothing good dwells; for to will is present with me, but how to perform what is good I do not find. For the good that I will to do, I do not do; but the evil I will not to do, that I practice. Now if I do what I will not to do, it is no longer I who do it, but sin that dwells in me. I find then a law, that evil is present with me, the one who wills to do good. For I delight in the law of God according to the inward man. But I see another law in my members, warring against the law of my mind, and bringing me into captivity to the law of sin, which is in my members. O wretched man that I am! Who will deliver me from this body of death? I thank

*God—through Jesus Christ our Lord! So then, with the mind*
*I myself serve the law of God, but with the flesh the law of sin*
(Romans 7:17-25).

It is in the mind that we wrestle with the spiritual and carnal nature. Because we have the power to choose, we find ourselves engaged in the daily battle of deciding between life and death. *"For to be carnally minded is death, but to be spiritually minded is life and peace"* (Rom. 8:6).

Many give their lives to Christ believing that all they have to do is attend church on Sunday, turn over all their problems to God, and subsequently, God will keep the conflict and they then get to go home to live free from their problems. Au contraire, it doesn't work like that. You can't just take your sin and your circumstances to the Lord and leave them in some mythical place, thinking that this will resolve the conflict. It is natural that when you give your life to Christ you want to be free of all your issues. You come to Him seeking peace and a refuge from the troubling storms of life that daily permeate your existence. You want to leave them somewhere far, far away. So, you take them to the altar to leave them with God. But, where is the altar if it is not in you?

The only altar on which you can lay your troubles is the altar within you. If God is in you, then He is the one who introduces the conflict in order that when you meet God at that place of surrender (the altar), He can begin to replace those things that have always caused conflict between your carnal or sinful desires and the will of the spirit. It is important to understand that your struggle is not with the devil; it is with God, for God has set you up, through the introduction of conflict into your life, in order to bring you to a place of maturity.

It is God who often initiates conflict in our lives (except for that self-induced conflict that comes from our own immaturity). Since God is in humanity, when we meet Him at the internal altar, it is in our own minds and hearts where God begins to replace the sinful desires that are inherent in us. How does He do that? He must replace the old mind with a new mind that will now desire spiritual things. In seeking Christ, we eventually discover the freedom we have always longed for.

## THE WAR WITHIN

In the mind you wrestle with the desires of the flesh that are engaged in serious war against the will of the spirit. When you first come to God, you feel powerful as you open yourself to Him, and at the same time, there is another dark part that is infringing on this new source of power. This is when the conflict reaches its peak—the conflict between good and evil, between right and wrong.

Often, God's people find themselves asking, "Why does it seem that this conflict has intensified, rather than diminished, since I met Christ?" You must understand that when Jesus becomes a part of your life, the *Light* that Christ shines on the mind illuminates and accentuates two opposing forces—the mind of the flesh and the mind of the spirit. At this time, your eyes automatically open to seeing the *Light* shining into your soul, and you now see yourself in the *Light* as never before. You begin to see your faults and human frailties juxtaposed between your weak nature and His powerful life that is at work within you.

In order to grasp the extent and energy released in the battle for the mind, we will turn to the Book of Romans 8:1-6 and 12:1-2. But we cannot just step into the middle of His Word to the Romans without understanding the context and content of the message of the letter the apostle Paul wrote to the Romans. It is critical to note that the apostle Paul was the first systematic theologian. His writing style was sequential and methodical; he developed the problem and then clearly established the solutions. The Book of Romans is the most comprehensive presentation that we have of the redeeming grace of God that has ever been written.

## ROMANS—THE FIFTH GOSPEL

The Book of Romans has been described as the greatest exposition of the Christian doctrine of soteriology (salvation) anywhere in Scripture. This Book is regarded in theological circles of discussion as Paul's treatise of the Gospel. Many theological scholars refer to the Book of Romans as the Fifth Gospel. In Martin Luther's Preface to the Epistle to the Romans, he writes, "This Epistle is in truth the chief part of the New Testament and the purest Gospel."¹ This Epistle contains an orderly, logical development of profound theological and spiritual truth. It illustrates ever so clearly and masterfully the plan of salvation and the development of the doctrine of righteousness by faith.

The most evident theme in the Book of Romans is the Gospel. Paul supports his credibility to write this Gospel in his opening words to the Romans as he declares that he was *"called to be an apostle and set apart for the gospel of God"* (Rom. 1:1 NIV). Proceeding from that point, he declares with great confidence his total faith in the Gospel message that has been committed to him. *"For I am not ashamed of the gospel of Christ: for it is the power of God unto salvation to every one that believeth, for the Jew first and also for the Gentile"* (Rom. 1:16 KJV).

Paul goes on to say, with sorrow in his heart, that this same Gospel was not accepted by all Israelites (see Rom. 10:16). At the same time, with joy, he announces that this Gospel graciously (and fortunately) includes the Gentiles (see Rom. 15:16). It is also in the Book of Romans that the righteousness of God is revealed from faith to faith (see Rom. 1:17), imputing through the Word that righteousness is accessed by faith and faith alone. Paul further maintains that the one who is righteous shall live by faith. Paul returns to the theme of faith over and over again. He positions faith in contradistinction to works, making it clear that faith, not human works, is the doorway to right living. Faith releases a heavenly power that enables us to walk right before God and to fulfill our destinies in this world.

Although some of the truths of the Book of Romans are quite profound in the depth of their mystical and spiritual reality, making it hard to grasp the expanse of their revelation, Paul presents God's basic plan of redemption in a clear and understandable way. If people open their hearts to the Holy Spirit, He will guide them into the truths that Paul lays before them.

In the Preface to the Letter of St. Paul to the Romans, Martin Luther wrote about the Book of Romans,

> It would be quite proper for a Christian, not only to know it by heart word for word, but also to study it daily, for it is the soul's daily bread. It can never be read or meditated too much and too

well. The more thoroughly it is treated, the more precious it becomes, and the better it tastes.[5]

Before moving on, we want to compare the Book of Romans to the Four Gospels—Matthew, Mark, Luke, and John. The four Gospels are historical books (describing Christ's unique birth, His unique teaching, and His unique life) with deep spiritual undertones. The Gospels present the man Jesus and the message that He brought from His Father to be relayed to the world. We learn much about God through the way Jesus interacted with the religious world and the way He intermingled with the common people. The four Gospels establish Christianity as more than a religion—more than simply a rule of life. Jesus came to establish a relationship with the human race. It is in the Gospels that we discover the *"theo-anthropicness"* of Christ—His *Deity* and His *humanity*. It is in the Gospels that people meet God face-to-face. The One who lived in the face of God now comes to exegete (explain) God to people. It is in the person of Christ and through His humanity that we are led into a divine experience where we encounter God. And it is in the historical/ geographical presentation of Christ by the four Gospel writers that the greatest difference between Christianity and any other religion in the world is established.

As we analyze and contrast the four Gospels to the Book of Romans, we find that the historical and geographical accounts of these Gospels bring us into the person of Jesus Christ by whom we gain our salvation. In the Gospels we meet Jesus, we hear His words, and we watch His actions. In the end, we see Him dying on a cross and then, with great joy, we read of the resurrection. In the Gospels, we see what He did, but it is in the Book of Romans that we come to understand the implications of what He did. In the Book of Romans, we ascend the high mountains of spiritual revelation and begin to see the significance of justification, propitiation, reconciliation, redemption, sanctification, and adoption. If we read only the four Gospels, we will never come to understand the spiritual significance of those actions. That is why the Book of Romans is considered to be the Fifth Gospel, for without it, the story of Jesus is simply another story; but with the Book of Romans, the glorious light of

Heaven shines into our souls as we are made aware of the heavenly reality of what Christ has done.

What the Epistle of Romans does is give us a theological and philosophical perspective of the Gospel so that believers can come to know Jesus fully. We enter into all the spiritual realities through our faith, and we are transformed by that faith.

## A TRIP DOWN THE ROMANS ROAD

In Romans chapter 1, Paul begins to build a solid case for the condemnation of all humankind because of humanity's reprobate behavior. In chapter 2, however, he directs focus toward the Jewish people and says:

> *You who make your boast in the law, do you dishonor God through breaking the law? For "the name of God is blasphemed among the Gentiles because of you," as it is written* (Romans 2:23-24).

The Jews, whom Paul had in mind, considered themselves not only separate from the Gentiles, but also felt they had a pure faith and that the Gentiles were ignorant in spiritual matters. They knew they had the truth and were proud of it. Paul saw these Jews as dangerously self-confident because they believed themselves to be called to be guides of the Gentiles, and they believed God's salvation belonged to the Jews (see John 4:22). In other words, Paul is saying, "Although you have the Mosaic Law, and you had God leading you from Egypt with a pillar of cloud and a pillar of fire, it does not make you better than the Gentiles." In essence, it is like saying to Christians, "You were born in church, but that does not make you any better than others, because you still don't do what God requires of you."

Paul's questions were designed to force the listener to realize that many did not understand God's law, had false confidence in it, and could not apply it readily to their daily lives. Paul urges that these religious Jews, who thought they were guides to the blind (Rom. 2:19—*"and are confident that you yourself are guide to the blind, a light to those in darkness"*), were actually breaking their own laws and dishonoring God (see Matt. 15:3-9).

Consequently, in Romans chapter 3, Paul declares that all are condemned; and he sums it up by saying:

*Even the righteousness of God, through faith in Jesus Christ, to all and on all who believe. For there is no difference; for all have sinned and fall short of the glory of God* (Romans 3:22-23).

In chapters 4, 5, and 6, Paul introduces justification by faith. Paul declares that you can no more justify yourself than Abraham could have a child at 100 and Sarah at 90. He illustrates the impossibility of justifying oneself using the example of this double impossibility—Abraham fathering a child at 100, impossible; Sarah giving birth to a child at 90, double impossible. So justification then could not be by works. Clearly, justification is by grace, and *grace cannot be minimized or reduced by sin.*

Thus, evil is not contradictory to grace as it is to the law; indeed, humanity's depravity makes their helpless evil behavior prerequisite for the grace of God. It is our powerlessness to change ourselves that qualifies us to receive the empowering presence that we call grace. It is because of grace that evil can never *outdo* God's goodness. It does not matter how bad or terrible we are, we can't "out evil" God's goodness.

Just as we are getting comfortable with God's grace and goodness, it is in chapter 7 that Paul introduces us to the struggle that all people have endured. With great pain and sorrow, he laments, *"Now if I do what I will not to do, it is no longer I who do it, but sin that dwells in me. I find then a law, that evil is present with me, the one who wills to do good"* (Rom. 7:20-21). This *now* brings the believer into the awareness of the quandary that whenever we would do good, evil is ever present. Humanity seems to be locked into an impossible conundrum. There appears to be no key to solving the puzzle of sin. The apostle Paul confirms here that there is always going to be a struggle; even with the matchless grace of God and with this enormous power working on our behalf, there is a constant battle with sins that have manifested themselves in the behavior of our flesh. Thus, as we battle with the flesh, trying to take on the divine nature of God, there is a fight and a struggle to walk in the promises of God.

Paul concludes in chapter 7 with the great question of the ages. *"O wretched man that I am! who shall deliver me from the body of this death?"* (Rom. 7:24) and then in verse 25 he makes this triumphant declaration, *"I thank God—through Jesus Christ our Lord. So then, with the mind I myself serve the law of God, but with the flesh the law of sin."*

In chapter 8, the apostle Paul introduces the universal principle of the law of the Spirit of life in Christ Jesus (see Rom. 8:1-2). Paul first declares that the Spirit of Christ assures victory and makes holiness possible through God's plan of redemption. It is in this chapter when we finally reach the summit or higher level of spiritual revelation as we come to understand that God has given His Holy Spirit to us as an enabler, a friend, and a source of power who will walk with us and help us overcome all things.

# PART ONE

# OUT OF THE BOX

How much happier you would be, how much more of you there would be, if the hammer of a higher God could smash your small cosmos, scattering the stars like spangles, and leave you in the open, free like other people to look up as well as down! As G.K. Chesterton wrote, "...As long as you have mystery, you have health; when you destroy mystery, you create morbidity."[1]

The first key to becoming a spiritual person is to get out of the box created by the various inputs into your life—religion, negative words spoken into your life, harmful experiences, failure, and your interactions with people—to name a few. Most of us don't even realize that we live within a confined compartment, but we are confronted with it every day when we are not able to think outside the paradigms that have been formed in our lives.

You will understand in this section that connecting to God and tearing down those paradigms is the only way to get out of the box. Allow the hammer of God to crush your little cosmos so that you can see the greater cosmos all around you. Once this happens, you will discover the freedom you always desired.

# CHAPTER ONE

# SURVIVING THE MIND FIELDS

The stage is set throughout the first seven chapters of Romans for the *therefore* that opens chapter 8. Paul states clearly that walking with God is not conflict-free. And it is significant to know that the apostle identifies two opposing forces in us—the force of the flesh, the law of sin and death; and the force of the Spirit, the law of the Spirit of life. These two forces are always in opposition to one another. It is in chapter 7 that we first find Paul sharing his personal feelings—which is, the law cannot save you from sin. Paul laments:

> *But I see another law in my members, warring against the law of my mind, and bringing me into captivity to the law of sin which is in my members. O wretched man that I am! Who will deliver me from this body of death? I thank God—through Jesus Christ our Lord...* (Romans 7:23-25).

## INTERNAL CONFLICT: OPPOSING FORCES

It is critical for us to recognize that the flesh and the Spirit are in constant conflict because the mind of sinful flesh sets its desires against the mind of the Spirit. Thus, the mind becomes the battleground of:

- *Grace* against law
- *God* against satan
- *Revelation* against situation
- *Spirit* against flesh

■ *Word* against the world

When opposing forces battle within the mind, you must understand that whoever or whatever controls your mind controls you. You are essentially mind. Thus, when you, as a Christian believer, begin to battle between the desires of the flesh and the will of the Spirit, it must be clear that satanic forces are trying to control your thinking through your flesh, which is connected to your five senses. At the same time, your faith in the Word of God is fighting the sensual perception of your situation. This is the battle that goes on in the mind.

Paul understood the struggle between flesh and Spirit, and in this text the apostle doesn't mince words; he goes straight to the conclusion and opens with *therefore*. *"There is therefore now no condemnation to them, which are in Christ Jesus"* (Rom. 8:1a). The Greek word for *condemnation—katakrima—*means "to speak against your experiences."[1] Condemnation (*katakrima*) makes believers feel negative about self in the midst of what God is doing for them in the struggle. Self-condemnatory thinking actually causes you to aid and abet the negative satanic forces that are working through your sensual perceptions in order to defeat your faith; guilt and faith are opposing forces.

Paul admonishes us to realize that these opposing forces have nothing to do with where we are in Christ. If we are believers, we are now "in Christ," and the Holy Spirit is guiding us through and out of our conflicts as He gradually releases us from the control of the flesh. He is also reminding us that we are not to despair or become discouraged while the Spirit is fighting to subdue the flesh.

It is important to note, however, that Romans 8:1 is often used to divide the Church into two groups—the group that walks according to the flesh and the group that walks according to the Spirit. This interpretation adds to the conflict of the mind because it perpetuates negative attitudes in some church-goers toward others when more established church members view less mature members as carnal—thus increasing the sense of inadequacy and causing a feeling of condemnation even though they are now in Christ.

A careful review of this Scripture, however, reveals that this is not the intent of Romans 8:1. Scriptures disclose that all believers have the promise that, although they still may stumble and fall into sin's power in their flesh, they will experience ultimate victory over sin as they mature in Christ. Maturity is now defined as the continued process of walking according to the Spirit while overcoming the flesh. We must, therefore, understand that new believers do not come into the house of God and jump from natural to spiritual without experiencing carnal battles with their sin nature. Every believer has to mature and, of course, has to grow in a relationship with God.

So then *"walk not after the flesh, but after the Spirit* [Greek: *peripateo me kata, sarx kata pneuma*]" (Rom. 8:4 KJV), is an adjectival clause describing *all* who are in Christ Jesus. It must be crystal clear that the battle being fought in the mind has nothing to do with your level of maturity as a Christian believer. You may be a babe in Christ or you may be spiritually mature in Christ, but the key is your *position* in Christ and not your level of maturity. So, everyone who is in Christ is to be walking according to the Spirit.

## IT'S IN THE MIND

As we seek deeper understanding of the text, it is critical to grasp the concepts in both Hebrew and Greek because, even though Paul wrote in Greek, many believe that his thoughts were influenced more in Hebrew. Moreover, Scripture show that it was through Paul that God gave us an extensive understanding of two languages and two mind-sets. As we search for deeper understanding, we find that the Hebrew thought is quite enveloping when it comes to the mind. Also, when we widen the parameter of this text to include Paul's thoughts in Hebrew, the word that is most used for "mind" is *nephesh*, and it means "life," "person," "soul," "creature," "appetite," and "mind."[2] Moreover, one writer said,

> The Mind is the only part of man (who is made in Yahweh's [God's] Image) or Yahweh Himself where the emotion, the character, the attitude, the spirit, the control, the reasoning, the creativity (by design or a plan), and where the intent of the heart take place. These are all evidences of the condition of the spirit (whether Holy or not) that resides within the mind.[3]

If you accept these concepts, then in your mind is:

- Your life

- Your soul

- Your appetite

- Your person

- YOU—the total person

Furthermore, in Hebrew, the etymological root of *nephesh* is "to breathe, or refresh one's self." This is evident in the creation of people because when God made people, He made a panoply (covering) of flesh from the dust of the ground, which was not alive until God blew breath into Adam. Thus, the life of people is housed within that panoply of flesh, and what is housed in the panoply of flesh is *nephesh*—the mind. This means that the mind, which is one's life, person, appetite, and creature is directly linked to God's breath. It is now God's breath inside this panoply of flesh. In other words, the soul (*nephesh*) of a person is connected to the very breath (*nephesh*) of God; as soon as you become a living soul, your spirit and mind are connected to God.

Likewise, when the Lord visited Adam in the cool of the day, He didn't visit his physicality (panopy of flesh), because his physicality was already given to Eve. God came to visit Adam's mind, which is also *nephesh*. He came to deal with what He had breathed (*nephesh*) into the man. Thus, any time the mind (*nephesh*) does not have the shackles of the flesh, it reaches for God. The writer says in Psalm 42:1, *"As the deer pants for the water brooks, so pants my soul [nephesh] for You, O God."*

Human beings have a natural knowledge of God; and John Calvin said,

> There is within the human mind, and indeed by natural instinct, an awareness of divinity.... God himself has planted in all men a certain understanding of His divine majesty. Not only has God sowed in man's minds that seed of religion, but has revealed Himself and daily discloses Himself in the whole workmanship of the universe.[*]

Similarly, prescientific Greek theories, which are rooted in theology, concentrate on the relationship between the mind and the soul, the supposed supernatural or divine essence of the human person. For example, Aristotle approached the concept of the soul from an essentially scientific perspective, employing elements of biology and metaphysics that encompassed everything from the concepts of substance, form, and matter, to those of potentiality and actuality.[5] Essentially, while Christians and other religious faiths have traditionally deemed the soul to be an immortal entity that lives on after physical death, Aristotle viewed the soul as united with the living body and, therefore, unable to exist without a host—the body. He also regarded the soul or mind as the truth of the body.[6] In essence, initially in God's primal creation of humanity, the body or the panoply of flesh was hosting the mind, but it was not antagonistic to the originally intended relationship of the mind with God. It was sin that contaminated the flesh and made it antagonistic or hostile to the relationship; thus, now the flesh, because of sin, has changed—as Aristotle would say—from being a host to now being a prison warden.

*Mind* is also the term most commonly used to describe the higher functions of the human brain, particularly those that are subjectively conscious, such as personality, thought, reason, memory, intelligence, and emotion. Modern Greek theories see the mind as a phenomenon of psychology, and the term is often used synonymously with consciousness.

The Greek concept of "mind" comes from the word *phroneo*, and it means "to set one's mind on a thing."[7] The Lord says, "You have to set your mind on things above, not on things on the earth" (see Col. 3:2). We must set our minds on things above because the mind is seeking to operate in the realm of its natural environment and not be controlled by the limitations of sinful flesh. Thus, the intent of the Spirit in its war against the flesh is to free your mind from being suffocated by the flesh.

# CHAPTER TWO

# CONNECTING TO GOD AND TO THE WORLD AROUND YOU

The apostle Paul tells us,

> *For to be carnally minded is death, but to be spiritually minded is life and peace. Because the carnal mind is enmity against God; for it is not subject to the law of God, nor indeed can be* (Romans 8:6-7).

When satan sends negative thoughts into your mind that make you feel inferior, he also condemns you and gives you guilty feelings of shame, depression, low self-esteem, and unworthiness. Yes, satan wants to gain control of your mind so he can influence your thoughts.

The question now becomes, "Why is the mind the battlefield for conflicts between flesh and Spirit?" God's Word describes two kinds of minds—the carnal (sensual, sinful, worldly, fleshly) and the spiritual (connected to and controlled by the Spirit of Christ). The carnal and sensual are synonymous terms used to keep you away from God; while at the same time, God is trying to control your mind by the Word through His Spirit, which is connected to your spirit by faith in the Word. It is also true that spiritual warfare is waged in the mind because it is the place where thinking, reasoning, understanding, and remembering take place. On the other hand, satan gets to your mind through your senses—that is, through the sensual perceptions of the flesh. He also uses your senses to deceive and control the mind. Hence, the carnal mind always listens to the desires of the flesh, while the spiritual mind is concerned about how the human spirit relates to God.

## TORMENTING THOUGHTS FROM THE TEMPTER

Descartes (1596-1650), a French philosopher, known as the father of modern philosophy, was convinced that the mind could be deceived. He maintained that demons could cause ideas to appear within his mind such that he was deceived, not only about the existence and nature of secondary qualities, such as mathematical abstracts, but even about the existence of things that involved only his senses, such as feeling, touching, seeing, tasting, and smelling. In order to do this, he said, "An evil genius would have to be deceiving him in everything he has ever known."[1]

We need to be aware that the circumstances we experience do not always leave us without vestiges or thoughts to remind us of our past experiences. It must be made clear that satan wants to fix it so that when you go through an adverse situation or circumstance, you pick up a negative idea that attaches itself and becomes embedded in your mind. On a personal level, satan wants control of *your mind* so that when you experience a personal crisis, you also experience depression or low self-esteem. These feelings then become attached, in your mind, to the personal crisis or situation. If you do not rid yourself of the tormenting thoughts of depression or low self-esteem that are now attached to the crisis you are going through in your mind, then when you have another personal crisis or circumstance, you are more likely to pick up additional tormenting thoughts.

For example, you may be experiencing a broken relationship caused by the death of a spouse or loved one, a divorce, or other forms of separation causing depression or guilt. Subsequently, you enter into another relationship before you are healed from the depression of the previous relationship. When this happens, you may find yourself picking up tormenting thoughts of worry, anxiety, nervousness, and other mental tormentors in a new relationship, while still dealing with the old tormenting thoughts—fear, guilt, and depression—that have been embedded in your mind from the previous relationship.

When looking at you from the outside, others may not see all the tormenting thoughts that are now attached to you and are imprinted in your mind. We don't always see the feelings of depression, guilt, or low self-esteem, or the scars from dishonesty and lack of trust. The problem is that you can look very good on the outside, while at the same time you can be totally weighed down by tormenting thoughts that have been imprinted in your mind.

It is critical for you as a Christian believer to understand that it is in the mind where the imprints of positive and negative experiences are embedded. And when you don't erase the negative experiences from the mind, it can lead to mental and emotional disorders. Satan realizes that if he can leave an indelible imprint on the mind, he can use your past experiences and mistakes to make you feel guilty in order to cripple your future.

Yes, satan is always trying to leave imprints of negative issues in your mind, and Paul warns us that,

> *"For what the law [Greek: nomos] could not do, in that it was weak [astheneo] through the flesh, God did by sending His own Son in the likeness of sinful flesh [homoioma hamartia sarx], on account of sin: He condemned sin in the flesh"* (Romans 8:3).

God wants you to have a spiritual mind so you can commune with Him. You must, therefore, comprehend that transformation from the flesh, which is the natural person to the spiritual person, takes place in the mind. Consequently, you must win the battle in your mind.

## REVELATION FROM THE REDEEMER

In addition to pleasant and unpleasant circumstances leaving imprints on your mind, satan will also insert thoughts of sexual impurity, lust, and mental sexual fantasies in your mind. It is during these times when you might wish that God would just disconnect your flesh. You might even say, "Lord, if this sinful flesh was not here, I wouldn't have these sensual feelings and desires to get me into trouble; so I wish You would just shut down the desires of my flesh." But God does not remove or shut down the desires of the flesh, because these are natural, God-given feelings. Instead,

He wants you to overcome, to manage, and to maintain control over your sensual feelings and desires. He wants you to learn to control your fleshly and sensual nature and bring it into subjection to the will of God.

Thus, when it seems that God is not helping you through the situation, He is actually sending the Word (*rhema*) from His Spirit to each believer's spirit. At this point, the Spirit of Christ is seeking to control your mind. In other words, God doesn't always change your situation; He changes your mind. If God would change your situation, while your mind remained unchanged, then you would still be attached to your mind and your mind attached to the situation, even though God had changed the situation. What God wants you to know is that if He changes your mind, then *you* can change your situation.

This is now switching the control of the mind from circumstance and sight to Word and Spirit, and therefore, it brings us face-to-face with the great controversy of dualism and monism. Monism (Greek: *Monos*, "single"), in philosophy, is a doctrine that says ultimate reality is entirely of one substance. On the other hand, dualism is the theological and philosophical concept in which the body and soul are made of two different substances. Descartes posits, "God created two classes of substance that make up the whole of reality: thinking substances (minds) and extended substances (bodies)" and Descartes proves that he himself must have the basic characteristic of thinking, and that this thinking thing (mind) is quite distinct from his body.[2]

Therefore, when you ask, "Why do I have to fight this battle?" The answer becomes clear: When opposing forces battle within the mind, it has to be understood that satanic forces are trying to control your thinking—your mind. In addition, at the same time as you are dealing with past situations and fighting battles, God is giving you revelation. Oh yes, God gives you revelation while you are fighting the battle between flesh and Spirit, and you have to look to God for revelation in order to keep your mind from being bound by past experiences and situations. The child of God does not rely on situation; the child of God lives by revelation.

Thus, your understanding of God's position in relationship to your faith is crucial to how you think, because when you are in right relationship with

God, your mind feeds on the Word and Spirit of Christ. And when you feed on His Word, God gives you critical revelation on how to change and control your mind. Furthermore, when God wants to renew your vision, He gives you revelation as He communicates to your mind—through faith in the Word. It is essential for you to understand that you are built in the image and likeness of God. God is Spirit, and He expresses His thoughts by communicating—His Spirit to your spirit—to your mind through the Word.

## CONNECTED TO THE WORLD THROUGH THE SENSES

In reviewing the third chapter of Genesis, we find that God created people in His own image. Yes, we are made in His image, but even though we are made in the image of God, we have certain limitations. We are limited by five senses, and it is through the five senses that we take in all the information that the mind can process. However, it must be crystal clear that our limitations do not hinder God, because our relationship with Him is through faith, not through our senses.

It is also in Genesis chapter 3 where we find that satan targeted the woman's sense of hearing by speaking with her and then focused on her sense of sight. First, the serpent said to the woman, *"You will not surely die* [heard his voice]*"* (Gen. 3:4). Eve listened and heard the voice of the serpent. Next:

> *When the woman saw* [looked] *that the tree was good for food, that it was pleasant to the eyes, and a tree desirable to make one wise, she took* [touched] *of it and ate* [tasted]. *Then, she also gave to her husband with her, and he ate* (Genesis 3:6).

To recap the event:

- Eve heard the voice of the serpent.
- Eve looked and saw the fruit.
- Eve touched the fruit.
- Eve tasted the fruit.
- Eve smelled the fruit as she was eating it.

## CONNECTED TO GOD THROUGH FAITH

*It is critical to note that while you are connected to the world through the senses,* you do not come to God through your senses. You have never seen or touched God, you have never smelled God—you don't know what cologne God wears—and you have never tasted God. (When the Bible talks about tasting God, it is metaphorical.) Thus, in order to have a relationship with God, you can come to Him only through faith and not through your senses. Why? Because the acceptance of salvation is based on faith in the Word—Jesus is Lord. Moreover, it is important to note that the Scripture also says that Christ is to be received by faith (see Col. 2:6-7).

Similarly, David Hume (1711-1776), Scottish historian and philosopher, believed that since we have never observed God directly, we have no experience by which to testify to His existence or nonexistence. Hume boldly claimed that, "Religion is therefore based entirely in faith, not in reason."[3]

Since it is impossible to scientifically prove whether God exists or not, you must make a leap of faith in proclaiming His existence. Also, as mentioned in Chapter One, Calvin wrote, "There is within the human mind, and indeed by natural instinct, an awareness of divinity."[4]

Moreover, Paul declares that faith is evoked as a response to the Gospel: *"So then faith comes by hearing* [the message], *and hearing by the Word of God"* (Rom. 10:17). Accordingly, faith is heard through the Word of Christ; *"...It pleased God through the foolishness of the message preached to save those who believe"* (1 Cor. 1:21). In essence, it is the hearing that produces faith, and the faith that saves is a faith that unites the believer to the Spirit of God. One writer maintained,

> Paul evidently looked to the proclamation of the "word of the Lord," the message about Christ, the Gospel, as being able in itself and by itself to evoke faith. Thus, the Gospel was by the power of God (itself a Divine Force) unto salvation.[5]

Faith then becomes the avenue by which you connect with God. It is also written, *"For by grace you have been saved through faith..."* (Eph. 2:8).

And since you are connected to the Spirit of God, you can depend upon God's Word to penetrate through horrific circumstances, bad situations, and failures of the past that are embedded in your mind.

## CHAPTER THREE

# THINKING AFFECTS YOUR TALKING AND WALKING

## EXPRESS YOURSELF

We learned in Chapter One that the Hebrew word for "mind" is *nephesh*, which refers to the inner mind. And in addition to the inner mind, there is also an outer part of the mind. This outer part of the mind is *peh* from the etymological root word *paah*, that is, "the mouth."[1] The Bible says, "*... Out of the abundance of the heart* [nephesh], *the mouth* [peh] *speaks*" (Matt. 12:34). The mouth is the expression of the outer side of the mind, which is the external manifestation of one's character and disposition. In essence, the mouth is the organ through which one's relationship with God is ascertained. God said, *"Believe in your heart"*—yes, and also—*"confess with your mouth* [peh]" (Rom. 10:9) because the mouth speaks.

The chief way that God has designed people to express themselves is through speech. "Speech is generated as we 1exhale the breath that is within us, and this breath is given shape as it passes over our vocal cords."[2]

You speak or express praise from the *peh* or outer part of the mind. However, before you can praise God, you must have a mind to praise Him. And when you set your mind on praising God, you set your life on it, your person on it; you set your whole being on it. When God sets His mind on something, He sets His mind on it through *your* mind. And when God's Spirit blows His thoughts into your mind, then the will of God must come to pass. When the Spirit of Christ moves in your life, you will no longer be manipulated through your flesh.

The thoughts of the mind are usually expressed through the words of the mouth; thus, anytime there is an expression through the mouth, there is first a thought in the spirit. Consequently, it is logical that expressive people are thinking people, and if you are not thinking, you have nothing to express. We can then assume that God talks much because He thinks much. And because God has so much to tell us, He blows His thoughts into our bodies to make us living thoughts. But even though God's thoughts are formed in people's spirits, neither the character nor the thoughts of people are evident until they are given expression from the people.

Descartes theorized in *Meditation III* that it is from God's breath that you get your ideas. Descartes believed that God caused the idea of God in his mind. As a result of his belief, Descartes then inquired into the subject of how he received this idea from God. He came to the conclusion that this idea is innate in him because, from the moment of his creation, God imposed the idea of Himself in the mind of Descartes, very much like a worker stamping his name to the product of his making.

Descartes further hypothesized that he apprehended this idea in the same intuitive way that he understood the fact of his own thinking existence. Interestingly, he did not deduce God's existence because he knew this immediately and intuitively. Descartes then concluded,

> The contemplation of the idea of God is the source of greatest happiness in life. Although he admits that this is incomparably less perfect than the contemplation of God in the life to come as faith suggests, it is a fact of experience that the contemplation of God provides great happiness.[3]

In comparison to what Descartes said, God is saying, "When I blow My Spirit into you, I AM going to release you from your flesh, because your flesh will kill your vision." When you are connected to God, you can reach into the Spirit and speak the Word to break the power of the enemy all around you.

## WORDS ARE THOUGHTS OF THE HEART

The Bible says, *"As he thinks in his heart, so is he..."* (Prov. 23:7). The Hebrew concept of "heart" is the word *leb*.[4] When the word *leb* is used in the Bible, every immaterial function of a person is attributed to that person's heart: *"As he thinks in his heart, so is he...."* This refers not to his face or to his physicality or flesh, but to what is happening on the inside of him—in his mind.

The heart or *leb* then becomes the biblical term for the totality of a person's inner or immaterial nature. In biblical literature, *heart* is believed to be the most frequently used term for a person's immaterial personality function as well as the most inclusive term.

Blaise Pascal (1623-1662), a French mathematician, physicist, and religious philosopher, advocated a religious doctrine that taught the experience of God through the heart rather than through reason.[5] So the heart has its own logic and its own reasons, which may be different from those reasons derived from the senses, but they are just as valid, because our innermost thoughts come from the heart. In essence, words are the voice of the heart.

## WALK ACCORDING TO THE SPIRIT AND LIVE

Another Hebrew word, *ruah*, means "wind or breath that is spacious." *Ruah* in the Old Testament is translated into the Greek word *pneuma*, and it means "air in motion"—the Holy Spirit.[6] Considering the Day of Pentecost, the Bible says,

> *When the Day of Pentecost had fully come, they were all with one accord in one place, and suddenly there came a sound from heaven as a rushing mighty wind, and it [He] filled the whole house where they were sitting. Then there appeared to them divided tongues, as of fire, and one sat upon each of them. And they were all filled with the Holy Spirit and began to speak with other tongues, as the Spirit gave them utterance* (Acts 2:1-4).

In order to understand the relationship between spirit and breath, it is imperative that you understand the relationship of the Father, the Son (Word), and the Holy Spirit (wind in motion). It's the Spirit of God who blows into your nostrils, who refreshes and brings new life to your mind. Thus, to maintain control of your mind, you have to be connected to the

Holy Spirit of God. The Holy Spirit is the key, and the law of the Spirit—not a written law—is the regulated principle of the Holy Spirit.

The law of the Spirit or, in other words, the regulative principle of the Holy Spirit, which exercises control over the life of the believer, provides energy from the Spirit that gives you a desire to come out of where you are and go where the Lord wants you to go. This energy comes from the Spirit of God and blows naturally into your mind. As the Lord blows His Spirit into you, the energy from His Spirit will take you higher into the next level. The Lord will blow into your spirit until you can tell the world and satan that:

- I am coming out; I can't stay in the box.

- I have to come out. I am tired of being restricted, held back.

- I am coming out of poverty, depression, and low self-esteem.

- I am out of the box.

- I will never be the same because I am moving in the power of my anointing.

- I am liberated.

- I am free.

- No weapon formed against me shall prosper.

You are now empowered to defeat satan and to walk according to the Spirit because the Spirit who raised Jesus from the dead is the same Spirit who is alive in each of us. Consequently, you are no longer restricted by the carnal mind; you are no longer under law, but are now under grace; you don't owe the flesh any favors at all, but you are debtors to the Holy Spirit because Jesus conquered the grave to purchase your redemption; Christ Jesus did it by the power of the Holy Spirit. That same Spirit is now available to you. Thus, you have an obligation to live according to the Spirit because you are now spiritually minded, and *"There is therefore now no condemnation to those who are in Christ Jesus..."* (Rom. 8:1).

CHAPTER FOUR

# FREEING YOURSELF FROM THE BOX

The apostle Paul boldly declares to all believers, *"There is therefore now no condemnation to those who are in Christ Jesus..."* (Rom. 8:1). If you are in Christ Jesus, God has breathed His Spirit into your soul—your mind (*nephesh*), and because your mind is connected to the Spirit of God, you are released to God's original intention for your life.

Consequently, your mind wants to be at home with the Spirit of God. It's like—"E.T., go home." You may recall the popular movie, *E.T.*, which was released in 1982. At one point in the movie, E.T. (an alien from another planet) had nothing else on his mind but to go home. He had a very interesting and enjoyable experience while visiting Earth; he was treated very well and was taken care of. But even though E.T. was living with a loving family and was adored by the children, he still was an alien away from his original home. The planet Earth was not E.T.'s original habitat, and even after having so much fun, he wanted to go back home to his own environment.

Just like E.T., you might be saying, "I know the world is all right, and there are some good things here, but there is something greater—my home. I am not currently able to do all of the things I am capable of, but I want to reach my full potential. I want to be released from this box of sinful flesh so that I can be all that God has called me to be and achieve everything that God has placed in my mind."

## I AM FREE—THE FLESH NO LONGER HOLDS ME

Because you are now "in Christ Jesus," no matter what environment you are placed in or where you may stay for a while, you will find that the flesh is never good enough. It is too restricting; your thoughts and your will have now been elevated beyond your situations. When you look at God's original intention for your life, you'll understand that your mind wants intimacy with God without the restriction of your flesh or your environment. Consequently, you will not be satisfied until you are released from the box of sinful flesh and your mind is connected to the Spirit of Christ.

With your spirit connected to the Spirit of Christ, you can now focus with a single mind that is "in Christ Jesus." And with this single mind in Christ Jesus, you can do whatever God has created you to do. Flesh creatures will not be able to distract you. Therefore, as soon as you begin to feel that releasing power of God, you can rise up out of your box of flesh and declare, "I shall have everything that is mine. I shall have what God said I can have." You can boldly make this declaration because the Bible says, *"But if the Spirit of Him who raised Jesus from the dead dwells in you, He who raised Christ from the dead will also give life to your mortal bodies through His Spirit who dwells in you"* (Rom. 8:11).

In order to release yourself from condemnation, however, you have to realize that the Spirit of God who raised Jesus from the dead is the same Spirit who is alive in you. It is significant that you understand this concept because when this thought becomes real in your mind, *you* will know that it is time for *you* to get control of your mind, get rid of the negative imprints, and move to the next level of your walk in the Spirit of Christ.

In addition, because it is in the mind where the real battle is fought, you have to personally maintain power over the flesh. At the same time, you must be aware that, while it is not easy to conquer the power of the flesh overnight, every believer has the ability, by connecting to the Spirit of God through the Word of God, to receive power over the flesh in order to win the battle in the mind. Moreover, when you are in Christ and have been released into the power of God, then you can walk in His Spirit because you are:

- Free to rise up above your circumstances

- Free to be a powerhouse in the middle of a dying world

- Free to speak things as they are and bring them to pass

- Free to express yourself in a world of contradictions
- Free to look up and declare, "The devil thought he had me, but God has set me free"

## REDEMPTION—THE PRICE HAS BEEN PAID

Now the questions become:

1. "How can I believe that the Lord can take me to the next level if I don't believe that I can go there myself?" and

2. "How can I believe that the Lord has forgiven me if I don't forgive myself?"

Both of these questions bring us back to the act of faith, and your action becomes the evidence of your faith. When you take a look at condemnation, you will find that it causes you to process negative thoughts about yourself, and when these thoughts are locked into your mind, you will not release yourself to the power that you have in Christ Jesus. As sinful people, we innately want to try to solve our every problem on our own, which is contradistinctive to the cry of the spirit person. It is also true that we are in the habit of thinking that we have to work things out for ourselves, which is inherent in our nature as sinful people—our punishment for Adam's sin. Even though, the concept of "let go and let God" has been intellectualized and thereby diminished, its spiritual impact can release you to the power that you have in Christ Jesus. It is through the Word that the Spirit of Christ releases all believers from bondage, while the flesh is fighting with the spirit.

The fact is, you are now free, and because of Jesus' death and resurrection you are entitled to complete justification, substitution, and sanctification. Look at the Lord's design of people and learn a great truth about the Father, Son, and Spirit. The spirit of a person is invisible, but it is this spirit that determines who a person is; essentially, your character is bound up in your spirit, and the Spirit of Christ wants to communicate with your spirit—your mind. Christ has redeemed you from the law of sin and death to the law of the Spirit of life in Christ. The primary condition of Christ's work in redemption is the incarnation of Christ Jesus who knew no sin, but was sent in the likeness of sinful flesh to die for humankind. He gave His life as the substitution for what the Law could not do, weak as it was through the flesh. God sent His own Son in the "likeness of sinful flesh" and as an offering for sin. We must, therefore, always emphasize that while the Son of God came "in flesh," He did not come in "flesh of sin," but in the "likeness of sinful flesh" (see Rom. 8:3).

## REUNITED WITH GOD

We must always remember that the mind longs to reunite with God, and we have to think through our circumstances as we think ourselves out of the bondage of our situations. Where the Spirit (*nephesh*) of the Lord is, there is liberty, and the mind (*nephesh*) longs to be free from being a slave to the flesh.

You have to now say, "Get the shackles off me. I am getting ready to break out because I am a child of God." You are coming out of the box of your sinful flesh and removing the shackles of your mind. You are coming out of the box because you want to know the will of God for your own life.

CHAPTER FIVE

# THEOLOGICAL AND PHILOSOPHICAL THOUGHTS AND CONCEPTS

## THE MIND IS THE SEAT OF ALL SPIRITUAL AND CARNAL EXPRESSIONS

| THEOLOGY | PHILOSOPHY |
|---|---|
| THEOLOGICAL VIEW—BODY AND SOUL | PHILOSOPHICAL CONCEPT—DUALISM |
| A traditional Christian's view is that the mind is a distinct reality. You have a soul, which is different from your body; your body will die and then your soul will go to Heaven or hell. | In philosophy of mind, dualism is a set of beliefs that begin with the claim that mental events and physical events are totally different kinds of events.[1] |
| The historical record of God's formation of man provides the key to an understanding of the essential nature of man.<br><br>Genesis 2:7—*"And the Lord God formed man of dust from the ground, and breathed into his nostrils the breath of life; and man became a living being."* | Issues and concerns of the "mind-body" dates back at least to Plato, who was considered the first dualist. Plato contends that the soul is distinct from the body and is capable of maintaining a separate existence from it. (Assumes the mind and body are two separate and distinct parts—material and immaterial).[2]<br><br>According to Descartes, God created two classes of substances that make up the whole of reality: thinking substances (minds) and extended substances (bodies).[3] |

| THEOLOGY | PHILOSOPHY |
|---|---|
| THEOLOGICAL VIEW—BODY AND SOUL | PHILOSOPHICAL CONCEPT—DUALISM |
| Other Scriptural references: | Descartes—"And although we suppose that God united a body to a soul so closely that it was impossible to form a more intimate union, and thus made a composite whole, the two substances would remain really distinct, notwithstanding this union."[4] |
| Romans 7:23-25—"But I see another law in my members, warring against the law of my mind, and bringing me into captivity to the law of sin, which is in my members. O wretched man that I am! Who will deliver me from this body of death? I thank God—through Jesus Christ our Lord! So then with the mind I myself serve the law of God, but with the flesh the law of sin." | |
| In relating his own personal experience as a Christian, Paul declares that he is carnal, a creature of the flesh, sold under sin, in captivity to sin; consequently, the indwelling depravity of human nature rebels against God's law. The good news is that because we have the law of the Spirit of life, we have the victory over the law of sin in the flesh. | Philo said that in the early ages a sharp distinction was made between the principles of good and evil. He thought that the spiritual part of man, his mind or soul, is the seat of good, and his body, the material part, is the seat of evil. Consequently, when the soul is incorporated in the body it suffers a fall from divine perfection and becomes predisposed to evil. Thus, the goal of man is freedom from matter and a return to God who is perfect goodness.[5] |
| Psalm 63:1—"O God, You are my God; early will I seek You; my soul thirsts for You; my flesh longs for You in a dry and thirsty land where there is no water." | Descartes—"If you would be a real seeker of truth, it is necessary that at least once in your life you doubt, as far as possible, all things."[6] |
| Ecclesiastes 12:7—"Then the dust will return to the earth as it was, and the spirit will return to God who gave it." | Saint Augustine—On the Immortality of the Soul, he said, "But the soul is present as a whole not only in the entire mass of a body, but also in every least part of the body at the same time."[7] |
| Matthew 10:28—"And do not fear those who kill the body but cannot kill the soul. But rather fear Him who is able to destroy both soul and body in hell." | John Calvin—French theologian and leader of Calvinism, "Seeing that a pilot steers the ship in which we sail, who will never allow to perish even in the midst of shipwrecks, there is no reason why our minds should be overwhelmed with fear and overcome with weariness."[8] |
| Romans 8:10—"And if Christ is in you, the body is dead because of sin, but the Spirit is life because of righteousness." | |

| THEOLOGY | PHILOSOPHY |
|---|---|
| THEOLOGICAL VIEW—BODY AND SOUL | PHILOSOPHICAL CONCEPT—DUALISM |
| Romans 12:1-2—*"I beseech you therefore, brethren, by the mercies of God, that you present your bodies a living sacrifice, holy, acceptable to God, which is your reasonable service. And do not be conformed to this world, but be transformed by the renewing of your mind, that you may prove what is that good and acceptable and perfect will of God."*<br><br>First Corinthians 5:5—*"Deliver such a one to satan for the destruction of the flesh, that his spirit may be saved in the day of Lord Jesus."*<br><br>Colossians 2:5—*"For though I am absent in the flesh, yet I am with you in spirit."*<br><br>Galatians 5:17-18—*"For the flesh lusts against the Spirit, and the Spirit against the flesh; and these are contrary to one another, so that you do not do the things that you wish. But if you are led by the Spirit, you are not under the law."* Paul is reminding us that because we are in Christ, we have control over sin in the flesh. Thus, when the flesh sets its desire against the Spirit, the law of the Spirit in Christ overrules the law of sin and death. Hence, we can win the battle of sin in the flesh in the mind.<br><br>Galatians 5:24-25—*"And those who are Christ's have crucified the flesh with its passions and desires. If we live in the Spirit, let us also walk in the Spirit."* He is declaring that when the Holy Spirit indwells us and we walk according to the Spirit, we have the power of the Holy Spirit to have victory over satan. | Saint Augustine—"My mind withdrew its thoughts from experience, extracting itself from the contradictory throng of sensuous images, that it might find out what that light was wherein it was bathed....And thus, with the flash of one hurried glance, it attained to the vision of That Which Is."[9]<br><br>Thomas Aquinas (an early Christian thinker)—"To achieve goodness is the highest good, and the greatest good for man is to realize God's purpose in the creation of man. The best way to attain goodness is to abandon worldly things and seek communion with God.... Evil is the absence of good and when an object fails to achieve good results, evil comes into being."[10]<br><br>Descartes—When asked, "How is it possible for an immaterial substance to come into contact with a material substance?" Descartes simply stated that he "inhabits his body like a pilot in a vessel; and that the body is strictly a mechanical and machine-like substance. Its functions are entirely different from those of the spirit. The spirit is synonymous with mind.... The mind serves as the director of the body."[11]<br><br>Blaise Pascal—"The immorality of the soul is something of such vital importance to us, affecting us so deeply, that one must have lost all feeling not to care about knowing the facts of the matter."[12]<br><br>J. Gresham Machen—"I think we ought to hold not only that man has a soul, but that it is important that he should know that he has a soul."[13] |

# MEANINGS AND EXPLANATIONS WITH USE AND APPLICATION

## CARNAL (Greek: sarx\sarx)

**Strong's Concordance #4561:** flesh (as stripped of the skin), i.e. bodily temporal, or animal, unregenerate: the body (as opposed to the soul {or spirit}, human nature with its frailties and passions).

**Vine's Expository Dictionary:** From *sarx,* "flesh," signifies "having the nature of flesh," i.e. sensual, controlled by animal appetites, governed by human nature, instead of by the Spirit of God. It is as the equivalent of "human," with the added idea of weakness, figuratively "of the weapons of spiritual warfare, of the flesh" or with the idea of unspirituality, of human wisdom, "fleshly," as in Second Corinthians 1:12; and "retaining to the flesh" (i.e., the body) as in Romans 15:27.

**Webster's Dictionary:** relating to or given to crude bodily pleasures and appetites; marked by sexuality; bodily, corporeal, temporal and worldly. The physical nature of human beings.

**Use and Application:** Be clear that any hostile or disobedient tendency toward God's Word comes out of carnal (fleshly) nature.

## CONDEMNATION (Greek: katakrima\kat-ak-ree-mah)

**Strong's Concordance #2631:** an adverse sentence (the verdict) to judge against.

**Vine's Expository Dictionary:** (cf. 2632), "to give judgment against, pass sentence upon; to condemn," implying (a) the fact of a crime; (b) the imputation of a crime, as in the "condemnation" of Christ by the Jews.

**Webster's Dictionary:** Censure, blame; the act of judicially condemning; the state of being condemned.

**Use and Application:** Understand that no matter how you may feel, Christ Jesus will not condemn you because you belong to Him. Jesus said, *"He who hears My word...has everlasting life, and shall not come into judgment, but has passed from death into life"* (John 5:24).

## LAW (Greek: nomos\nom-os)

**Strong's Concordance #3551:** through the idea of prescriptive usage, (regulation), spec. (of Moses; also of the Gospel), or figuratively a (principle): law.

**Vine's Expository Dictionary:** To divide out, distribute, primarily meant "that which is assigned"; "usage, custom," as decreed by a state and set up as the standard for administration of justice.

**Webster's Dictionary:** A binding custom or practice of a community; a rule of conduct or action prescribed or formally recognized as binding or enforced by a controlling authority.

**Use and Application:** The law here does not refer to God's written moral commands in the Old Testament, but to the system of operation that the Spirit of life, the Holy Spirit, carries out in our lives, breaking the dominion of the old law (principle) of sin and death. (Reference the Spirit-filled Bible commentary notes.)

## MIND (Greek: phroneo\fro-eh)

**Strong's Concordance #5426:** to exercise the mind, i.e. entertain or have a sentiment or opinion; by implication to be (mentally) disposed (more or less earnestly in a certain direction) from. *"phren"* (#5424) to interest oneself in (with concern or obedience): set the affection on, (be) careful, be like, be of one, be of the same, let this mind (regard, savor, think).

**Vine's Expository Dictionary:** "To think, to be minded in a certain way"; (b) "to think of, be mindful of." It implies moral interest or reflection, not mere unreasoning opinion. In Romans 8:5, *"they that are after the flesh) do mind (the things of the flesh)"*; literally means "minding the same," and "set (not) your mind on," things of the flesh.

**Use and Application:** When the mind is renewed by the Holy Spirit, the whole mind is set to have understanding, be wise; to feel, to think to have an opinion of one's self, think of one's self, to be modest, not let one's opinion (though just) of himself exceed the bounds of modesty; to think or judge what one's opinion is; to be of the same mind, i.e., agreed together, cherish the same views, be harmonious; to direct one's mind to a thing, and to seek, to strive for.

## MIND (Greek: phronema\fron-ay-mah)

**Strong's Concordance #5427:** From *phroneo* (#2426); (mental) inclination or purpose: (be, be carnally, be spiritually) mind.

**Vine's Expository Dictionary:** Denotes "what one has in the mind, the thought" (the content of the process expressed in *phroneo*, "to have in mind, to think"); or "an object of thought."

**Use and Application:** What one has in the mind, the thoughts, and the purposes. The verb behind "set their minds," refers to the basic orientation, bent, and thought patterns of the mind rather than to the mind or intellect itself (Greek: *nous*). It includes a person's affections and will, as well as the person's reasoning. Paul uses the same verb in Philippians, where he admonishes believers to "have this attitude [mind] in yourselves which was also in Christ Jesus" (see Phil. 2:5).

# PRACTICAL APPLICATIONS

There is a struggle to walk in the promises of God because there is a constant battle for control of the mind. When we accept Christ Jesus into our lives as Lord and Savior, there is an internal struggle between two forces—the law of sin and death and the law of the Spirit of life. In essence, accepting Jesus actually introduces us to internal conflict because the carnal mind (the mind of the flesh) sets its desires against the mind of the Spirit. So walking with God is not conflict-free because there is a constant battle for control of the mind.

It is important that you think of some specific applications and reflections to apply both the theological and philosophical lessons learned to correctly understand:

- The mind is the seat of carnal and spiritual expressions, and you are to walk according to the Spirit.

- *"There is therefore now no condemnation...,"* (Rom. 8:1) means Jesus not only paid the debt of sin, but also cleansed us *"from all unrighteousness"* (1 John 1:9).

Even though Christian believers are no longer under the dominion of sin, we will always experience conflicts with sin in this present life. However, we have the promise that although we still stumble and fall into sin's power in our flesh, we will experience ultimate victory over sin.

## ACTION STEPS

Actions to take or things to do in order to apply faith to defeat satan and to walk according to the Spirit:

A. Seek God with all your heart and with all your soul.

1.  Begin by praising God for what He has already done.

2.  Meditate on what God is saying in the Scripture (read Romans 8:1-13) and ask the Holy Spirit to lead you in prayer for guidance and understanding of God's Word.

3.  Ask God for what you want. With prayer and supplication, let your request be known. Ask the Holy Spirit to reveal God's truth and the will of God for you.

4.  Worship God in Spirit and in Truth, and commit yourself to being transformed by the Word.

5.  Make a commitment to spend at least 30 minutes a day alone with God.

6.  Make a commitment to fast and pray at least one day each week.

7.  Pray and praise God again—just give Him thanks and praise.

B. Begin each day in the reality that you are a new creature and that the Spirit of Christ dwells in you and that you are no longer under condemnation for past sins.

C. Pray inwardly for the Lord to open your mind and understanding so you can learn the practical characteristics of a mind that is walking according to the Spirit and not according to the flesh.

D. Spend time reading and studying God's Word.

1.  Prayerfully and carefully read John 14:17 to understand that the mind that is directed toward truth is aware that the Spirit of Christ dwells (lives) in you and that you are to be aware that you are always in His presence.

2.  Read Galatians 6:8 to understand how to please God by sowing seeds for the harvest.

3.  Sow the Word in order to win souls by sharing the Gospel and telling others of God's love, grace, and mercy. Note: living evangelistically is not only a privilege; it is rewarding.

The following Scriptures are valuable tools for guiding others to salvation: John 3:16; Romans 10:9-10; and Acts 4:12.

## PERSONAL GROWTH AND DEVELOPMENT

The most important thing that you can do to walk according to the Spirit is to read and study the Word daily. Walking according to the Spirit and being controlled by the Spirit of Christ does not happen through osmosis; it comes by being obedient to His Word. That is by studying and applying the Scripture until it is written on your heart and in your mind.

The following Scriptures are valuable tools for understanding that *love* fulfills the law when you are walking according to the Spirit: Romans 15:14; First Corinthians 12:7-8; Galatians 5:16-26; Colossians 3:12-16; and John 15:2.

Pray and ask the Holy Spirit to lead you in prayer for guidance, repentance, and thanksgiving.

One way to guide your prayer is to remember the acronym ACTS:

A= Adoration or honor for God

C = Confession of your sins

T = Thanksgiving and praise for what God has done

S = Supplication/Intercession (praying for the needs of others)

## READ, RECORD, REFLECT

To gain more from your time in the Scripture, you should read and reread the passage.

You must know what the passage says before you can understand what it means and how it applies to you and your ministry. You should:

- Read to determine, "What does this passage say to me?" Begin by reading the passage to determine what the Scripture is all about.

- Record what you see. It is extremely important that you write some notes and keep a record of your insights and questions.

- Mark unfamiliar words or phrases that you do not understand, and write your answers in your journal or study notes.

# PART TWO

# FINDING YOUR ORIGINAL SELF

Who am I? That is the question all of us ask ourselves. It is easy to get lost in the busyness of life so that in the end it is our activity that defines who we are. That's why so many people become addicted to their work. They are seeking to establish their identity from what they do instead of who they are. Whether you are a businessperson or a stay-at-home mom, it is easy to allow your identity to be defined by what you do.

Jesus came to establish the uniqueness of who we are, not based upon works, but upon creation. In His inaugural message, Jesus reversed the natural order of perceptions, making it clear that what is inside a person determines the man or woman, not what that person appears to be on the outside. In this section, we will help you refocus and end the masquerade so you can discover your original self.

# CHAPTER SIX

# I AM AN ORIGINAL

## A ONE AND ONLY

You are an original, and you cannot be duplicated, imitated, or destroyed. You can, therefore, walk in the world, but not be governed by the environment and standards of the world. You have been created by God. The world can scrape through all the façade and look at the beautiful, powerful, joyful you—God's original and new creation.

There is no one like you in the whole wide world; no one has your DNA, your fingerprints, or your voice print. As we consider what it means to be an original, we turn our attention to the apostle Paul's appeal for renewing the mind found in Romans chapter 12:

> *I beseech you therefore, brethren, by the mercies of God, that ye present your bodies a living sacrifice, holy, acceptable unto God, which is your reasonable service. And be not conformed to this world: but be ye transformed by the renewing of your mind, that ye may prove what is that good, and acceptable, and perfect, will of God* (Romans 12:1-2 KJV).

These verses introduce the transition from the theological presentation of the Gospel to what is called exaltation—and that is to move us from those things that God has done for us into how we should respond. So it is in the beginning of Romans chapter 12 that Paul urges us to measure our lives to our beliefs.

## CONNECTED TO LIFE OR DISCONNECTED AND DYING

We will compare and contrast the differences between a conformed mind (to copy) and a transformed mind (to create). Interestingly, the comparison can be illustrated by the remarkable differences between the water in a pond and the water in a river. The water in a river constantly moves and flows, while water in a pond is stagnated or stilled. A river is connected to other bodies of water; thus water moves in and out. This continuous movement indicates that changes are constantly taking place or that the water is living.

A pond, on the other hand, is a detached body of water; it stands alone. Because there is no continuous flow of water entering or leaving the pond, the water in it is often stagnated, and when water is stilled and stagnated, it stinks with dead and decaying matter.

As we further ponder the analogy of a river and pond, we can compare it to ourselves being connected to a life source—the Spirit of Christ, which flows through a person's faith—the belief in Christ Jesus, into that person's spirit. However, if the person is not connected to the life source, then the mind is not being refreshed and renewed. And when the mind is not being refreshed, it becomes stale and causes one to act or react in ways that are not symbolic of who one really is.

When your life is stale, there is no creativity because your mind is stilled and stagnated. Nothing happens in a stale life but more depression. It is significant then to understand the mind from the Hebrew concept of *nephesh* mentioned earlier, which regards the mind as being life, soul, creature, person, and appetite. The original or etymological root of the Hebrew word *nephesh* is to breathe, to refresh oneself. The mind becomes the very core of the individual; it's your inner self, your heart, and your person—it's you.

Again, the Hebrew term for "spirit"—*ruah*, is a metaphorical term to describe an activity or vitality; it has the same meaning as the Greek term, *pneuma*, which means wind or breath. According to Scripture, the *ruah*, *pneuma*, or the Holy Spirit is the "the physical breath of life" (see Gen. 2:7; 6:17; 7:15).

Because you are now connected to the Spirit of Christ, the Living Water, your mind is being renewed and refreshed with the original and creative breath or wind from the Holy Spirit of God. Essentially, God's Spirit (breath) is flowing into your spirit, and consequently, you are constantly being transformed by the renewing of the mind to be more and more like Christ Jesus. Thus, you are now called to live a different lifestyle than what the world offers. You are not to conform to the world's values of selfishness, corruption, unethical behavior, and customs.

It is critical for you to understand that there has to be a personal connection to the life source—the Holy Spirit (*ruah* or *pneuma*)—the "breath" or "wind" of life—flowing through faith into your spirit and then into your mind, which is symbolic of who you are. The mind then becomes the very essence of who you are. Thus, everyone can say, "My mind is my inner self; it's my heart; it's my soul; it's my appetite; it's my total person; it's who I am."

It is in the mind where the Spirit of God transforms or spawns creativity. Creativity does not take place from outside the mind; rather, we create from an inner personal connection to the very breath of God. Therefore, when we are not connected to the Living Water, our lives become stale as stilled water in a stagnated pond. And when our lives are stale, there is no creativity; nothing happens when life is stale or dying.

As long as you are living, your body is always generating new cells. No matter how old a person is, the body is constantly renewing itself because renewal is a part of the life process. On the other hand, anyone who is not renewing is dead, and dead things are completely controlled by the environment. Dead people cannot tell you what to do with their bodies; they cannot argue; neither can they resist.

Likewise, people who no longer have the strength to stand on their own connection to their life source then seek to find strength in conforming (being like everybody else). Whenever people live according to the dictates of others, they cannot connect to the will of God for their own lives. Therefore, they have a greater propensity to become more of a copy than an original.

## THE LIVING WATER

It is significant to understand the concept that Christ Jesus projects when He declares, *"If anyone thirsts, let him come to Me and drink. He who believes in Me, as the Scripture has said, out of his heart [belly] will flow rivers of living water"* (John 7:37-38). Jesus is saying that it doesn't matter what your environment is; it doesn't matter what's going on around you. If you are connected to Him, everything that has bogged you down and stalemated you is now flowing out of you because He is pouring His life back into you.

Understanding that Christ is the flowing river of Living Water can be compared to water being central to Israel's whole economy and existence. During biblical times, the rabbis taught the principles of water and rain. Water was a very important part of the Feast of Tabernacles and the holy days of Sukkot. (It was during this festival time that Jesus Christ said, *"If anyone thirsts, let him come to Me and drink"* [John 7:37].)

By way of illustration, the priest would pour the water over the altar to signify Israel's gratitude for the rain that had produced the harvest and would pray for rain in the coming months. The priest would recite a hymn of praise:

> And in that day you will say: "Oh Lord, I will praise You; though You were angry with me, Your anger is turned away, and You comfort me. Behold, God is my salvation, I will trust and not be afraid; for YAH [the shorter form for the Lord's holy name Yahweh, or Jehovah], the Lord is my strength and song; He also has become my salvation. Therefore, with joy you will draw water from the wells of salvation" (Isaiah 12:1-3).

And so, in exchange for our bodies as a living sacrifice, the Spirit of the Lord is saying to each of us, "I am pouring life back into you." And as God's Spirit flows through your mind, He is transforming you into a new creature. You are now one of God's original creations. You have a renewed mind.

It is important to understand that because God renews from the inside, He prevents you from adapting to the circumstances and situations that could affect you from the outside. It is this new life source flowing through your mind that strengthens you to become defiant in the face of adversity. You are enabled to stand no matter how great the environmental influences because He has delivered you from being dead in sin. God wants a living sacrifice, not a dead one.

We must always be mindful that the flesh may desire to conform to the world and to be like someone else—so much so that most don't even know who they are because they have not tapped into the Source of life that flows as Living water. This constant flow from the life source refreshes your mind and prevents you from conforming, thus allowing you to be creative. When you are connected to the life source, you no longer live your life the way the world wants you to live. You now live the way God intends you to live.

CHAPTER SEVEN

# HOW TO CHANGE YOURSELF

Have you felt trapped in a situation, somewhere you did not want to be, and then all of a sudden you broke free by the power of your own intuition, by the power of your connection with God? If so, then you understand that there is nothing more refreshing than being liberated, delivered, and set free from a relationship or from being tied to someone who has been controlling your mind and maintaining dominion over you.

There is nothing more liberating than standing on your own two feet with security in your faith in God, knowing that the Spirit of Christ is flowing through you. He has liberated you from conforming to the sinful desires of a carnal mind so that satan and his demons no longer have dominion over your mind. And as God is flowing through you, He wants to glorify Himself in you.

Now that you are transformed and have a new mind, you can dictate to your environment. God has created you to have dominion over your environment. However, God wants each one of us to have control over self before having dominion over the environment.

It is quite important to note that, while God created you to have dominion over the environment, He did not create you to have control over me, nor did He create me to have control over you. In fact, one writer said, "God the creator never intended man to rule over or dominate his own, but rather to rule the creation and resources of earth."[1]

## CHANGED FROM THE INSIDE

Yes, you have been transformed by the renewing of your mind, and God's Spirit (breath) is flowing into your spirit so that you can maintain control over your carnal and sinful desires of the flesh so that your mind can become more and more like Christ Jesus. In order for transformation to take place, however, a *change* must occur. The word *change* has a variety of meanings; some dictionary definitions of change include: to become different or undergo alternation; to undergo transformation or transition; to go from one phase to another to make different in form; to transform, to give and take reciprocally; to become different.

Early philosophers objected to the notion of *change* being real because they believed that "something that is, cannot come to be," and since they believed that something cannot come from nothing, they maintained that change is impossible. Aristotle, on the other hand, discarded this concept by introducing the notions of defining *change* in a thing as "the passage from potentiality to actuality." Aristotle used this concept in physics to explain potential energy (energy at rest, dead, and not moving) and kinetic energy (energy in motion, alive, flowing, and changing).[2]

When applying Aristotle's concept of change to transforming the mind, we can say that during the process of being transformed by the renewing of our minds, a *change* occurs. Our minds change from carnal to spirit. However, the renewal and *change* can take place only because we are connected to the source of power—the Living Water—the Spirit of Christ.

To change from potentiality (wanting to be in Christ) to actuality (being in Christ), there must be an internal or external force (the Holy Spirit) or pressure applied for you to realize your ability to change from the state of potential to one of actual being. The Spirit of Christ is the power that transforms, changes, and moves you from potentiality (being conformed) to actuality (being transformed) by the renewing of your mind.

Change can be temporary; examples include going on vacation for two weeks, rearranging the furniture, changing the color of your hair, or going on a diet and losing 20 pounds. Change can also be long-term or permanent. Once your birthday comes, you will never go back to a younger age. When you reach the age of 21, you can never go back to age 19 or 20. A permanent or eternal change is making a commitment to

Christ as Lord and Savior. So being transformed by the renewing of the mind is a permanent change and a commitment to being personally connected to the Spirit of Christ in order to walk according to the Spirit.

John Wesley described the change that God worked in his heart through his faith in Christ: "I felt my heart strangely warmed. I felt I did trust in Christ, Christ alone for salvation, and an assurance was given me that He had taken away my sins, even mine, and saved me from the law of sin and death."[3]

When you have a personal connection to the Holy Spirit of God, He constantly transforms and renews you, taking you from being a potential child of God and changing you into an actual child of God. In essence, you are now renewed and transformed from potentiality (being controlled by the carnal and sinful nature) to actuality (being in Christ and walking according to the will of the Spirit) because Christ Jesus gave His life to release you from the law of sin and death. You are a new and original creation, and everything you have copied from others and incorporated into your mind is now dead or must die.

With your transformed mind, you can now expect to win all the battles in your mind because during the transformation process, God blew—and He is still blowing—a winning spirit into your mind. With the Spirit of Christ connected to your spirit, you can win every mind game that satan tries to play because holiness now controls your mind—your life, your appetite, and your sexual desires.

## GOD IS OUR MATERIAL AND SPIRITUAL SUPPLY

God is now your material and spiritual source of life. Scripture gives us specific incidences when God provided the Israelites with material prosperity that they did not work for. If you consider Deuteronomy 6:10-12, for example, you will see that God had to remind the Israelites that they were not to forget:

> *So it shall be, when the Lord your God brings you into the land of which He swore to your fathers, to Abraham, Isaac, and Jacob, to give you large and beautiful cities which you did not build, houses full of all good things, which you did not fill,*

*hewn-out wells, which you did not dig, vineyards, and olive
trees which you did not plant—when you have eaten and are
full—then beware, lest you forget the Lord who brought you
out of the land of Egypt, from the house of bondage* (Deuteronomy 6:10-12).

They were blessed with houses they did not build, food they did not
harvest, vineyards and olive trees they did not plant, and water from wells
they did not dig. Yet God still had to remind them that they were not to
forget their spiritual source of blessing when their physical needs were satisfied. We can see this same principle at work in several other places in
Scripture as well as in our lives today.

God supplies our needs in a wilderness where there is nothing. Even in
the midst of sickness, poverty, trials, tribulations, and all troublesome circumstances and barren surroundings, because when we look to the hills for
our help, our help comes from the Lord (see Ps. 121:1). It is that new life
source from the Spirit of Christ that flows through your mind that makes
you defiant in the face of adversity. You have the Holy Spirit, and the Bible
says, *"For the law of the Spirit of life in Christ Jesus has made me free from
the law of sin and death"* (Rom. 8:2).

## GOD WANTS A PERSONAL RELATIONSHIP WITH YOU

Yes, you can stand no matter how satan tries to influence your life. You
are to live your life the way God intends you to live—according to His
perfect will. You no longer want to live according to the desires of the flesh
and the dictates of the world. Specifically, when you are able to stand and
face the trials and tribulations in your life, then God is saying through His
Spirit to your mind:

- "I like your uniqueness because I created you so I can dwell
  in you."

- "I like what I made, and I want to move through you."

- "I want you to come out of the flesh and take your place in
  My Spirit."

- "I have had a relationship with somebody like you, but I want to communicate with the real you."

Furthermore, you can continue to stand because Christ Jesus prayed that you would not be removed from the world, but that you would be kept from the evil of the world (see John 17:15). You must, therefore, renew yourself constantly, because renewal is a part of the life process, and as long as you are living, your body is generating new cells from the source of life—the Spirit of Christ, which flows as Living Water.

With the Spirit of Christ flowing through your body as Living Water, He establishes an atmosphere in you that has nothing to do with the atmosphere outside; God deals with your mind from the inside. When we consider this concept theologically and philosophically, we know that our relationship with God has to begin within each person. The question then becomes, "Why do I look for God within myself?" The answer: "He indwells my spirit; I talk to God from the inside—spirit-to-Spirit. His Spirit transforms and renews my mind to be more and more like Christ Jesus. And with the mind of Christ, my mind reveals an attitude of love, joy, peace, long-suffering, kindness, goodness, faithfulness, gentleness, and self-control—that's inside."

## WE PERCEIVE GOD BY FAITH

Clearly, our relationship with God is not just physical, material, or intellectual; our relationship with God is spiritual; and the Spirit is life, and life is mind. Accordingly, John Calvin (1509-64), a prominent advocate of the *five solas* of the Reformation who reorganized organized religion and created a worldwide protestant movement, maintained, "There is within the human mind, and indeed by natural instinct, an awareness of divinity....God himself has implanted in all men a certain understanding of His divine majesty." Closely related to this *sensus divinitatis* (sense of divinity) is an external witness or revelation of God in creation. "Not only," writes Calvin, has God "sowed in men's minds that seed of religion of which we have spoken but revealed Himself and daily disclosesHimself in the whole workmanship of the universe. As a consequence, men cannot open their eyes without being compelled to see Him."[4] Hence, we look to God, not from the outside, but we look to God from within.

As God's Spirit indwells your spirit, His Spirit transforms and renews your mind to be more and more like Christ Jesus, and with the mind of Christ you, therefore, possess a natural knowledge of God that is revealed through faith. You now have a relationship of faith and reason because you come to God, who is a God of *reason*, only through *faith*.

Beginning with the first commandment, we find evidence for faith and reason. The verse states, *"And you shall love the Lord your God with all your heart, with all your soul, with all your mind, and with all your strength..."* (Mark 12:30).

We can, therefore, say that faith is the divine work in us, and it changes us from sin and death to life in Christ. When we have God in our minds, His Spirit controls our attitudes and behaviors, and when the Spirit of Christ is in control, we don't walk around seeking to be like everyone else around us, and we are not to be conformed to the world. As Christian believers, we are now seeking to be who we really are as the Holy Spirit is transforming and renewing our minds, so we may prove what is that good and acceptable and perfect will of God.

While it is true that you are saved through faith, there are two presuppositions for you to accept Him: You have to believe there is a God, and you have to believe that God rewards those who sincerely seek Him. According to Saint Augustine, "Faith is to believe what you do not see; the reward of this faith is to see what you believe."[5] Thus, you have to know about God in order to accept Him by faith. It is also critical that you understand that faith does not negate reason; it overrides reason.

Furthermore, A.M. Hunter wrote, "For St. Paul the Christian era is 'the dispensation of the Spirit,' the signs of which are 'freedom,' 'power' and 'joy.'"[6] So he sets the Christian life—its beginning, its middle, and its end—in the context of "the Spirit." Remember, our relationship with God is not physical, not material, not even intellectual; our relationship with God is spiritual.

You are to personally understand that God wants to communicate with you because He values your mind. Moreover, you are created in the image of God. This includes, among other attributes, the ability to reason; hence God also tells you,

> *"Come now, and let us reason together," says the Lord, "Though your sins are like scarlet, they shall be white as snow; though they are red like crimson, they shall be as wool"* (Isaiah 1:18).

It is clear that the conflict is not between faith and reason, but between faith and sight.

## CHAPTER EIGHT

# THE MASQUERADE IS OVER!

In order to understand both the negative and positive roles of the body in the spiritual life, and in life generally, we must take a deeper view of the nature of human personality, character, and action. It is quite evident that our environment teaches us to act like others around us. "Monkey see, monkey do," goes the proverb. It has also been proven that our environment influences personality development by as much as 50 percent, and it is largely for the good. But it also embeds in us habits of evil that permeate all human lives. This then influences the standard human patterns of responding to *"The lust of the flesh, the lust of the eyes, and the pride of life,"* which the apostle John said, *"is not of the Father but is of the world"* (1 John 2:16).

When you allow your mind to be conformed to the world, you then forsake the standard that God has established. Scripture tells us that God cautions in Jeremiah 2:13, *"For My people have committed two evils: They have forsaken Me, the fountain of living waters, and hewn themselves cisterns—broken cisterns that can hold no water."* Thus, sinful practices become the avenue for conforming to unacceptable standards and committing evil against God. Sinful practices become habits, then choices, and finally the character or the core of who you really are.

Remember, other people may try to control you so you will conform to their desires. They might try to manipulate you in order to control you, until you become totally helpless under the bombardment of their thoughts, their concepts, and their desires. When this happens, you become lost in what other people expect of you until you no longer expect anything of yourself. You begin to act more like the person who is in control of your mind; you begin to take on the world's mannerisms, the world's speech, the world's attitudes until those things co-occupy your mind with so much of what they are that you don't even know that you have lost your original self—the real you.

## CONFORMING TO CONTROLLING FORCES

Do you remember the last conversation you had when you were in the middle of a battle and you said something that was completely out of character for you? You may have even used expressions and acted in ways that are not characteristic of you. Then you heard yourself say, "I am sorry; that was not really me." Who was it? You were expressing something that did not come from within; it came from your association, but it did not come from you. You did something that did not come from your mind. In essence, you were not expressing the power of who you are.

Likewise, you may have been involved in a relationship where you acted in ways that you didn't even know yourself. You may have asked yourself, "Why did this happen to me?" The answer is, you became totally helpless because of the bombardment of other people's thoughts, concepts, and desires.

Subsequently, you realized that you took on an outward expression that did not come from the inside of you. And this is the crux of the word *conform*—it is not representative of the inner heart life. The prefix *con*, meaning "with" or "together," added to the Latin verb *formare*, meaning "to form," conveys the idea of assuming an expression that is patterned after something else.

Meanwhile, you may ask yourself another question: "How can I have any peace when I have allowed someone else to disconnect me from my mind and then try to connect me to his or her controlling forces?" It must be crystal clear that when you disconnect yourself from your mind and begin to focus on doing what the other person wants, you are then conforming your life and copying someone else.

This becomes complicated because, when you are not connected to the Spirit of Christ, you will assume the world's disposition, conforming to what others dictate. Consequently, when you give up your mind to the dictates of someone else, you become something that is not you. When you allow this to happen, the other person, while living and controlling his or her own destiny, is at the same time also controlling your mind and your destiny.

For example, two people are in an intimate relationship, such as marriage, and the relationship lasts for a long period of time. The partners become so attached to each other until they are of one mind. Then one person says, "I no longer need you," and the relationship ends. The query becomes, "Where do you go to get your original mind if you don't even know who you are?" You must be aware that when you give someone else control of your mind, you no longer have control of your life and destiny.

So, if you are not in control of your own mind, you are being controlled—according to the definition of *conformed*—by something or someone else. That means you are living a masquerade; you have picked up and copied the world's mannerisms, speech, expressions, and style. In essence, the other person's habits, attitude, and disposition have become embedded in your mind. You have been conformed to the world's behaviors and standards.

## RENEWED, REFRESHED, AND IN CONTROL

It is no secret that satan wants to control your innermost being and co-occupy your mind without you realizing that he is stealing the real, innermost being out of you. He seeks to make you more like him and his demons of the world. Yes, satan wants to control and manipulate every child of God. You must, therefore, be connected to the Living Water—the Spirit of Christ—who renews, refreshes, and transforms your mind so others cannot control you.

When you are transformed by the renewing of the mind, you can feel a wind blowing in your spirit as the Holy Spirit moves through your mind. And even though satan may attempt to control you, you will stand up and defy your environment because the Spirit of Christ is moving in you. And because you are connected to God's Spirit, you will resist conformity to the world and embrace the transformation that comes from Jesus Christ.

Nevertheless, you must keep in mind that this transformation process does not happen overnight. So you will not express outwardly as quickly as what takes place on the inside. When God places something in your mind, it takes time for the environment to adjust to who you are. Again, if you are "in Christ," you are a new creature; old things have passed away (see 2 Cor. 5:17). You are in Christ, and you have a new life, new attitude, new dreams, new power, new visions; you are now walking in the power of God. As an original, living with a renewed mind, you are no longer a clone of anyone else.

Moreover, it is with confidence that you can boldly say to the devil, "I don't need you. There was a time when I was under your control, and my broken spirit could not hold the water. When I tried to do what you wanted me to do, I got nowhere. When I tried to take on your mannerisms and sound like you, my mind was still stuck in sinful flesh. But now that I am in Christ, I am connected to the Living Water. I will not forsake the fountain of Living Water, and will not hewn for myself cisterns—broken cisterns that can hold no water."

Just think about David fighting Goliath and the mistake he would have made if he had put on Saul's armor. David knew that he could not wear Saul's armor into battle because it did not fit him. The only weapon he had was a slingshot—but an anointed slingshot. He needed nothing else. David was aware that he was connected to the Spirit of God and that God ordered his steps. He did not need Saul's armor, nor did he need Goliath's sword. David knew that he did not have to adapt the mannerisms of his enemies. God had a plan, and David walked in His will. It was David who said, "I can walk through the valley of the shadow of death and fear no evil" (see Ps. 23). He did not have to worry, for he was anointed with oil—the Holy Spirit. The Living Water was refreshing, renewing, and controlling his mind.

The Spirit of Christ, which indwells each believer, will cause you to bless others if you will be a living sacrifice of service. In Romans 12:1, Paul begged for the mercies of God because he saw the Light, the creative force, and he recognized that the Light in Christ is now embedded in the souls of people. In other words, he is really saying, "I beg you, I beg you, please, I beg you by the mercies of God." With a new and transformed mind, you are as alive as a river of water, and you are not stale and stagnated like a pond. You can feel the Spirit of Christ—an original branch that is attached to the Vine; then you know that you are transformed with a renewed mind.

To comprehend the power of the mind that has been transformed and renewed, it is critical to understand the word *transfigured*. The Greek verb *metamorphoo* is translated "transfigure" in the transfiguration narrative of Matthew 17:2 and Mark 9:2. The Scripture says that Jesus, the man of sorrow just like everybody else, walked up the mountain, and all of a sudden, He released in His mind the deity that He was. The Bible says that His body began to shine like the noonday sun (see Matt. 17:1-2). It was not a reflection of anything else; it was who He was on the inside. The only other place where the word *transfigured* appears in the New Testament is Second Corinthians 3:18, which mentions believers being *changed* into the likeness of Christ from one degree of glory to another by the operation of the Lord, who is the Spirit.

Remember, God created us for Himself, and He wants to bring out the beauties that He instilled in each of us. God wants us to know that He created each one of us as an original, and we belong to Him first. You must, therefore, open the valves of faith and keep hope alive in your transformed and renewed mind. Just as light overtakes darkness, you can overtake this world system when you are "in Christ." God now wants His Living Water to flow within your mind so that goodness will flow from you like water from a pellucid spring. You must stir your faith and stay connected to God's Spirit through God's Word.

## CHAPTER NINE

# THE POWER OF A RENEWED MIND

God does not work through conformity. He is looking for evidence of real transformation—transformation that takes place only through the renewing of the mind. When the mind is renewed, you have the "mind of Christ" (see Phil. 2:5-8). With God's Spirit constantly flowing into your spirit, you will find that you are becoming more and more like Jesus. And by having the mind of Christ, you will also have some "I AMness." Scripture records Jesus boldly saying, "I AM the Truth; I AM the Light; I AM the Vine. I AM, I AM, I AM" (see John 14:6; 9:5; 15:1). The "I AMness" separates Him from everyone else. He was unique in His birth, life, and resurrection. He did not conform His life to the customs and traditions of the culture during His life on earth. For example, it was against the custom and traditions when He spoke with the woman at the well and healed the sick on the Sabbath (see John 4; Matt. 12:9-14).

Likewise, when you have the mind of Christ, you will step into your "I AMness" and do what is not necessarily politically correct or traditional. We must walk in the Spirit, not in the flesh; be in the world, but not of the world. Then we can boldly say in our "I AMness":

- I am released from satan and his demons.
- I am going to be what God created me to be.
- I am growing by the power of God, and the real me is about to be released.
- I am totally original; I am not a copy, and I cannot be duplicated.

- I am going to overcome.

- I am an original blessing from God.

- I am going to stand up and claim what is mine.

- I am winning this battle in my mind because God put winning in my spirit.

Moreover, the mind is set on a higher level because we are renewed through our connection with the Holy Spirit. Then each of us can say, "Get the shackles off me. I am breaking out of these chains because I have been transformed by the renewing of my mind." Consequently, satan no longer has control over you because the chains have been broken. You have stepped into the world, but you are not conformed to the world. You are transformed by the renewing of your mind, and with the Spirit of Christ connected to your spirit, you are a new creature—an original, who cannot be imitated or duplicated. *You* are in control of *your mind*.

You have victory in your mind, power in your mind, joy in your mind, and you are climbing to higher heights. You can walk in the world, but not be governed by the environment and standards of the world. You have been created by God, and the world can scrape through all the façade and look at the beautiful, powerful, joyful you—God's original and new creation.

## YOU HAVE THE VICTORY

You are now walking in power because you have been transformed. The Spirit of the Lord is blowing into your spirit, and you are able to stand and defy your environment. It does not matter that you were once the greatest slave to satan and his demons. Satan can no longer control you because the fountain of Living Water is so far down in you that the devil cannot reach it.

With the Spirit of God connected to your mind, you have victory, and you shall overcome and have peace. You will have peace because the Bible says, *"You will keep him in perfect peace whose mind is stayed on You..."* (Isa. 26:3). God came and gave His life so that we might have life and have it more abundantly (see John 10:10).

Just remember, when you were bound by the world's attitudes and mannerisms, Jesus died and shed His blood to release you from sin and death. He went to hell and took the keys; then He stuck them in your hands and said, "Now, you open your own doors, you fix what's broken, and you straighten it out. I gave you the keys because I have made you like Me." You are now an emancipator and are slated for victory. You can boldly say, "I am expected to win the battle in my mind; I am running with all my heart, and I am going to overcome and win because God put winning in my mind."

## CHAPTER TEN

# THEOLOGICAL AND PHILOSOPHICAL THOUGHTS AND CONCEPTS

| WE PERCEIVE GOD BY FAITH—THE HEART, NOT BY REASON | |
|---|---|
| **THEOLOGY** | **PHILOSOPHY** |
| The Bible gives us clarity to support the concept in both the Old and New Testaments. Scripture reveals that God is a God of reason, and He wants to communicate with us; however, God is Spirit, and we can come to God only in spirit and truth. | The origin of the argument "reasons for faith" is witnessed by an early challenge from Epicurus, a Greek philosopher of the 3rd century B.C. Epicurus claimed that all order and design in the universes arose from accidental joining of atoms; the Designer of the universe was "blind chance." Cicero retorted: "If anyone supposes that this most beautiful and glorious world was made by the accidental coming together of atoms, I do not understand why he should not suppose that the Annals of Ennius might be produced by pouring out on the earth the twenty-one letters of the alphabets in countless profusion."[1] |
| **REASON** | |
| Isaiah 1:18—"'Come now, and let us reason together,' says the Lord, 'Though your sins are as scarlet, they will be white as snow; though they are red like crimson, they will be like wool.'" (NASB) | |
| Daniel 2:20—"Let the name of God be blessed forever and ever, for wisdom and power belong to Him" (NASB) | |
| First Corinthians 1:21—"For since in the wisdom of God the world through its wisdom did not come to know God, God was well-pleased through the foolish- ness of the message preached to save those who believe" (NASB) | |

## WE PERCEIVE GOD BY FAITH—THE HEART, NOT BY REASON

| THEOLOGY | PHILOSOPHY |
|---|---|
| **FAITH**<br><br>Hebrew 11:6—*"But without faith it is impossible to please Him, for he who comes to God must believe that He is, and that He is a re- warder of those who diligently seek Him."*<br><br>Ephesians 2:8—*"For by grace you have been saved through faith, and that not of your- selves; it is the gift of God."*<br><br>First Peter 3:15—*"But sanctify the Lord God in your hearts, and always be ready to give a defense to everyone who asks you a reason for the hope that is in you, with meekness and fear."* | A more philosophical argument for the existence of God is the Cosmological Argument, which is based on causality; the cause and effect relationship, to demonstrate the need for a subsistent (self-existent, uncreated) Being as the Initial Cause of all other things."[2]<br><br>Blaise Pascal—"It is the heart which perceives God and not the reason. That is what faith is: God perceived by the heart, not by the reason."[3]<br><br>Martin Luther—"All who call on God in true faith, earnestly from the heart, will certainly be heard, and will receive what they have asked and desired."[4]<br><br>Pascal—Thus wishing to appear openly to those who seek Him with all their heart and hidden from those who shun Him with all their heart, He has qualified our knowledge of Him by giving signs which can be seen by those who seek Him and not by those who do not. "Belief is a wise wager. Granted that faith cannot be proved, what harm will come to you if you gamble on its truth and it proves false? If you gain, you gain all; if you lose, you lose nothing. Wager, then, without hesitation, that He exists."[5]<br><br>Albert Einstein—"That deep emotional conviction of the presence of a superior reasoning power, which is revealed in the incomprehensible universe, forms my idea of God."[6]<br><br>Einstein—"I want to know all God's thoughts; all the rest are just details."[7] |

| WE PERCEIVE GOD BY FAITH—THE HEART, NOT BY REASON | |
| THEOLOGY | PHILOSOPHY |
| --- | --- |
| | Einstein—"My religion consists of a humble admiration of the illimitable superior spirit who reveals himself in the slight details we are able to perceive with our fail and feeble mind."[8] |
| | Saint Augustine—"Faith is to believe what you do not see; the reward of this faith is to see what you believe."[9] |
| | Saint Augustine—"Seek not to understand that you may believe, but believe that you may understand."[10] |
| | Saint Augustine—"Faith is a living, daring confidence in God's grace, so sure and certain that a man could stake his life on it a thousand times."[11] |
| | Paul Tillich—"Faith consists in being vitally concerned with that ultimate reality to which I give the symbolical name of God. Whoever reflects earnestly on the meaning of life is on the verge of an act of faith."[12] |

# MEANINGS AND EXPLANATIONS WITH USE AND APPLICATION

### BESEECH (Greek: Parakaleo\par-ak-al-eh)

**Strong's Concordance #3870:** to call near, i.e. invite, invoke (by imploration, exhortation or consolation): beseech, call for, (be of good) comfort, desire, (give) exhort (-ation), entreat, pray.

**Vine's Expository Dictionary:** Denotes "to call to one's side," hence, "to call to one's aid."

**Webster's Dictionary:** To beg for urgently or anxiously; to request earnestly; to implore; to make supplication.

**Use and Application:** *Beseech* is to call to one's aid. It is used for every kind of calling to a person that is meant to produce a particular effect, hence, with various meanings, such as "comfort, exhort, desire, call for," in addition to its significance "to beseech," which has a stronger force than to ask. The law says, "I command you," but grace says, "I beseech you."

### CONFORMED (Greek: suschematizo\soos-khay-mat-id-zo)

**Strong's Concordance # 4964:** To fashion alike, i.e. conform to the same pattern; conform to, fashion self according to. Denoting union; with or together; i.e. by association, companionship, process, resemblance, possession.

**Vine's Expository Dictionary:** "To fashion or shape one thing like another,"…This verb has more especial reference to that which is transitory, changeable, unstable; to that which is essential in character and thus complete or durable, not merely a form or outline.

**Webster's Dictionary:** To give the same shape, outline, or contour to: bring into harmony or accord; to be similar or identical or to act in accordance with prevailing standards or customs.

**Use and Application:** To conform one's self (i.e. one's mind and character) to another's pattern (fashion one's self according to). "Be not conformed." Paul is saying, "Don't let the world squeeze you into its mold!" Don't be molded by the mannerisms, speech, expressions, styles, and habits of this world! Kenneth Wuest has paraphrased the verse as follows: "Stop assuming an outward expression which is patterned after this world, an expression which does not come from, nor is it representative of what you are in your inner being as a regenerated child of God."[1]

## HOLY (Greek: hagios\hag-ee-oss)

**Strong's Concordance #40:** The state of purity, and it always refers to sanctification, sacred, pure, blameless, consecrated: (most) holy (one, thing), saint.

**Vine's Expository Dictionary:** Fundamentally signifies "separated" (among the Greeks, dedicated to the gods), and hence, in Scripture in its moral and spiritual significance, separated from sin and, therefore, consecrated to God, sacred. It is predicated of God (as the absolutely "Holy" One, in His purity, majesty, and glory).

**Webster's Dictionary:** Exalted or worthy of complete devotion as one perfect in goodness and righteousness; divine, for the Lord our God is holy; devoted entirely to deity or the work of deity; and having a divine quality.

**Use and Application:** A holy God calls for a holy people. Holiness is separation from everything profane and defiling; and at the same time, it is dedication to everything holy and pure. People or even objects, such as anointing oil or vessels, may be considered holy to the Lord—set apart for God's holy will and service. God's people are "saints," set apart for the service of the King of kings! Do you see yourself as a holy servant of the Most High God?

## MERCY /MERCIES (Greek: oiktirmos\oyk-tir-mos)

**Strong's Concordance #3628:** To have pity on; compassion, mercy; bowels in which compassion resides, a heart of compassion; emotions, longings, manifestations of pity. The point established is that the "mercy" and compassion shown by God are determined by nothing external to His attributes. By the "mercies of God"—this is not the same word for mercy which is found in Romans 11:30-32, but the idea is similar. It means "pity, mercy, compassion."

**Vine's Expository Dictionary:** "Pity, compassion for the ills of others," is used (a) of God, Who is *"the Father of mercies,"* 2 Cor. 1:3; His "mercies" are the ground upon which believers are to present their bodies a living sacrifice, holy acceptable to God, as their reasonable service, Romans 12:1.

**Webster's Dictionary:** price paid, wages; compassion that forbears punishment even when justice demands it; a blessing that is an act of divine favor or compassion; grace of God.

**Use and Application:** God has been so compassionate and merciful to us, and He wants us to show mercy and compassion toward all who are weak and defenseless. God sets the example by His constant compassion for the helpless and undeserving (see Isa. 54:8,10).

## MIND (Greek: Nous\nooce)

**Strong's Concordance #3563:** Verb "to know," it denotes the faculty of knowing, the seat of understanding, reasoning, and thinking ability. From the base of *ginosko* (#1097) form of the primary verb; "to know."

**Vine's Expository Dictionary:** Denotes speaking generally, the seat of reflective consciousness, comprising the faculties of perception and understanding, and those of feeling, judging and determining. Its use in the New Testament may be analyzed as the faculty of knowing, the seat of understanding, counsels, purpose, (of the mind of God; of the thoughts and counsels of God).

**Webster's Dictionary:** the element or complex of elements in an individual that feels, perceives, thinks, wills, and esp. reasons.

**Use and Application:** Your mind can only be renewed through the creative work of the Holy Spirit when your spirit is connected to the Spirit through the Word or study of the Scriptures.

## PRESENT YOUR BODIES
### (Greek: paristemi\par-is-tay-mee)

**Strong's Concordance #3936:** from beside to stand, i.e. (trans.) to exhibit, offer, (spec.) recommend, (fig.) substantiate; or (intrans.) to be at hand (or ready) aid: assist, bring before, command, commend, give presently, present, prove, provide, sew, stand before, by, here, up, with), yield.

**Vine's Expository Dictionary:** Denotes, when used transitively, "to place beside" (para, "by," histemi, "to set"), "to present," e.g. Romans 6:13 "yield."

**Webster's Dictionary:** to bring or introduce into the presence of someone esp. of superior rank or status; to give or bestow formally; to lay (as a charge) before a court as an object of inquiry; and to offer to view.

**Use and Application:** "Present your bodies." When you give God your body, you are giving Him all that you are and all that you have. The verb *present* is in the aorist tense, which simply means *"Do it!"*

## RENEW, RENEWING
### (Greek: Anakainosis\an-ak-ah ee-no-sis)

**Strong's Concordance #342:** renovation: renewing; new; freshness; regenerate.

**Vine's Expository Dictionary:** akin to "make new," a renewal is used in Romans 12:2, "the renewing (of your mind)," i.e., the adjustment of the moral and spiritual vision and thinking to the mind of God, which is designed to have a transforming effect on the life.

**Webster's Dictionary:** To make new spiritually: regenerate: to restore to existence; to make extensive changes in; and to begin again.

**Use and Application:** The renewing of the mind is the adjustment of the moral and spiritual vision and thinking to the mind of God, which is designed to have a transforming effect upon the life. This passage stresses the willing response on the part of the believer.

## SACRIFICE (Greek: thusia\thoo-see-ah)

**Strong's Concordance #2378:** From (#2380) to rush (breathe hard, blow, smoke), i.e. (by impl.) to sacrifice; to immolate (slaughter for any purpose); kill, do sacrifice, slay; from sacrifice (the act or the victim, literally or figuratively).

**Vine's Expository Dictionary:** Primarily denotes "the act of offering"; then, objectively, "that which is offered" of animal or other "sacrifices," as offered under the Law; of Christ, in His "sacrifice" on the cross; of the body of the believer, presented to God as a living "sacrifice."

**Webster's Dictionary:** An act of offering to a deity something precious.

**Use and Application:** When we think of sacrifice, it usually suggests merely an inconvenience or the giving of a costly gift. In Hebrew it involves the offering of a life.

## TRANSFORMED\TRANSFORM
## (Greek: metamorphoo\ met-am-or-fro)

**Strong's Concordance #3339:** (lit. or fig.) "metamorphose" change, transfigure, transform; to fashion (through the idea of adjustment of parts); shape; fig. Nature – form.

**Vine's Expository Dictionary:** (lit. transfigure) "to change into another form" (*meta,* implying change, and *morph,* "form"). Is used in the passive voice (a) of Christ's transfiguration.

**Webster's Dictionary:** To change in composition or structure; to change the outward form or appearance; to change in character or condition: convert; to become transformed: change—transformable.

**Use and Application:** Transformed: This is the ancient Greek word *metamorphoo*—describing a metamorphosis. The same word is used to describe Jesus in His transfiguration (see Mark 9:2-3). This is a glorious transformation! To be transformed, however, denotes renewal; "the renewing (of your mind);" the adjustment of the moral and spiritual vision and thinking to the mind of God, which is designed to have a transforming effect upon the life. The transformation process that takes place in the believer's mind causes you to become more and more conformed to the image of Christ.

## WORLD (Greek: aion\ahee-ohn)

**Strong's Concordance #165:** "An age, a period of time," marked in the New Testament usage by spiritual or moral characteristics, is sometimes translated "world"; the RV marg. always has "age." In Second Corinthians 4:4, we learn that satan is the "god of this world (age)." Christ gave Himself for our sins, that He might deliver us from this present evil world (age), Galatians 1:4. When we were unsaved we were a part of this evil, satanic age/world, but God has delivered us out of it.

**Vine's Expository Dictionary:** "An age, a period of time," marked in the New Testament usage by spiritual or spiritual characteristics, is sometimes translated "world." In Romans 12:2, "world" is relating to its fashion.

**Webster's Dictionary:** Human existence, an earthly state of human existence; life after death—used with a qualifier [the next]; the earth with its inhabitants and all things upon it; individual course of life.

**Use and Application:** As a believer, you are taught by grace to live godly in this present age. We are *in* this world, but we are not to live as those who are *of* this world and who are part of this world system, which is in opposition to the true and living God.

# PRACTICAL APPLICATIONS

It is clear that with a transformed and renewed mind you are laying aside your own desires to be of service. *"But do not forget to do good, and to share, for with such sacrifices God is well pleased"* (Heb. 13:16). It is important that you think of some specific applications and reflections to apply both the theological and philosophical lessons learned to correctly understand:

- Your connection to God is based on faith, not reason.

- The conflict is not between faith and reason, but between faith and sight.

- Transformation takes place in the mind.

## ACTION STEPS

Actions to take or things you can do in order let God's Word and His Holy Spirit maintain control of your transformed and renewed mind:

A. Prayerfully and carefully read Romans 12:1-2 and Hebrews 10:19-25.

B.  Show that you have faith by believing in God's promises, because God will do what He says He will do:

1. Celebrate daily that you have gained access to God through the shed blood of Jesus Christ. Tell others what God has done or is doing in your life and give thanks to God for everything—even the small things.

2. Have complete confidence and belief in God. Let the Word shape your thinking. Apply God's Word directly to your situations—insert your name in the text as you read the Scripture, and let the Word speak directly to you and your specific situations and issues.

3. Do not worry. Pray and trust God; He will fulfill His promises, even when you don't see any evidence.

4. Seek God diligently through prayer and meditation, and believe that He will reward you for it.

5. Practice persistent and patient praise.

6. Sing a hymn or song that reminds you to trust and praise Him for guiding you: *"Let us continually offer the sacrifice of praise to God, that is the fruit of your lips giving thanks to His name"* (Heb. 13:15).

7. Read First Peter 2:5 to understand that by the renewing of your mind, your body is now a temple—a spiritual house, a thank-offering to God.

8. Read Romans 12:1-2 to understand that with your new mind, your relationship to the world has changed.

9. Behave like a Christian in every part of your life—job, activities, recreation, attitudes, giving, shopping, dancing, eating, and talking.

## PERSONAL GROWTH AND DEVELOPMENT

- Spend daily time with God through the Word.
- Pray and meditate upon God's Word that your basic thinking patterns are being changed and that you gain the mind of Christ.
- Seek God's will so you know what He wants, and then do what is good and pleasing to God.

You are called to a different lifestyle than what the world offers with its behaviors and customs. You are now living according to the essential nature of the spiritual mind; hence, you are now required to:

- Love without hypocrisy

- Abhor what is evil

- Cling to what is good

- Be kind and affectionate to one another

- Serve the Lord

- Rejoice in hope and be patient in tribulation

- Pray continually

- Give to the needs of others

- Live peacefully with others

- Love your enemy

A.  Read and memorize Mark 12:29-31 and First Peter 3:15. Remember, God gave you a mind, and He expects you to use it.

B.  Read and study the Word so that you can glorify God by sharing the Gospel with others.

C.  Memorize verses from the Scriptures so you are always ready to give a testimony and defense to everyone who asks for the reason you have hope (faith) in God.

D.  Believe that Jesus is Lord, so you can say, as C.S. Lewis said, "I believe in Christianity as I believe that the sun has risen; not only because I see it, but because by it I see everything else."[1]

E. Live your life and govern your actions by your belief; it is through faith that you have committed yourself to Christ, and He is your personal Savior.

F.  The following Scriptures are valuable tools for assurance that faith is your personal trust in God: Romans 1:17; 3:22; 14:22; 2 Corinthians 5:7; Galatians 3:5; Ephesians 2:8; 6:16; 2 Timothy 4:7; 1 Peter 3:15; 1 Corinthians 1:21; and Isaiah 1:18.

G. Other Scripture references for understanding and experiencing transformation from the inside out: Romans 8:28-29; 12:1-2; 1 John 1:5-6; John 13:35; 1 Corinthians 2; 2 Corinthians 10:3-4; and Ephesians 4:22-24.

# SECTION TWO

# ENJOYING FREEDOM
# IN CHRIST

# A NEW MODEL FOR THE MIND—TRUTH FROM THE BOOK OF PHILIPPIANS

We begin Parts Three and Four by noting that in Philippians chapters 2 and 4, Paul is very conscious to leave us with the lesson of the strength and power (*dunamis* and *exousia*) of the mind. Paul says to the Philippians, *"Let this mind be in you which was also in Christ Jesus"* (Phil. 2:5).

The Book of Philippians is a book of rejoicing, of giving God accolades and of giving God praise. While writing this book of joy and rejoicing, Paul was incarcerated and was waiting to face Nero, that egomaniac and narcissist fellow. Eventually, because of the judgment of Nero, Paul was martyred for the cause of Christ Jesus.

Even at this very critical time in his life, Paul continues to write to a group of people who are free and proclaims to them the joy that they ought to have because of their relationship with God. The apostle Paul also conveys his love and gratitude for the believers at Philippi, as well as exhorting them to a lifestyle of unity, holiness, and joy.

Philippians is filled with commendation, encouragement, gratitude, love, and joy. At the same time, this book provides practical application for thanksgiving, rejoicing, and praising the Lord in the midst of adverse circumstances. Paul is also seeking to correct a problem with disunity and rivalry by urging all believers to imitate Christ in His humility and servanthood. He instructs that we are to be of the same mind, rejoice always, and pray about everything. When you follow the instructions given to the

Church, you will experience true joy by putting *Jesus* first, *others* second, and *you* last. Hence, JOY = Jesus, Others, You.

As the apostle urges believers to have the same mind (attitude) as Christ, he reveals much about Jesus Christ as the Son of God as well as Jesus Christ as Lord. Jesus is presented as the model of true humility as He willingly laid aside His heavenly glory to come to earth and die.

We must understand that His incarnation, humiliation, and obedience not only led Him to the cross, but also ultimately exalted Him to the highest place and gave Him a name that is above all names. God said,

> *At the name of Jesus every knee should bow, of those in heaven, and of those on earth, and of those under the earth, and that every tongue should confess that Jesus Christ is Lord, to the glory of God the Father* (Philippians 2:10-11).

From a historical perspective, the theme of the Book of Philippians is the "all sufficiency of Christ" (Greek: *autarkeia*). The Greek concept is self-satisfaction or always enough. Paul could therefore say, "I don't have to worry about anything; I can rejoice because God is always enough."

Paul was obviously so deeply rooted in God that, no matter what was happening in his life, he kept his mind on Christ Jesus. It is important to note that Paul's life was sharply divided into two parts by his conversion. Before his conversion, he was a furious persecutor of Christians, but his life was overturned when Christ appeared to him on his way to Damascus. He immediately lost his sight, and after three days of blindness, he was told that he would suffer many things for Christ's sake (see Acts 9:15-16). Besides the many persecutions, Paul also had to bear an infirmity or a thorn in the flesh (see 2 Cor. 12:7). In addition, he was bitten by a poisonous snake (see Acts 28:3). Paul summarized many of his other sufferings:

> *From the Jews five times I received forty stripes minus one. Three times I was beaten with rods; once I was stoned; three times I was shipwrecked; a night and a day I have been in the deep; in journeys often, in perils of waters, in perils of robbers, in perils of my own countrymen, in perils of the Gentiles, in perils in the city, in perils in the wilderness, in perils in the sea, in perils among false*

*brethrens; in weariness and toil, a sleeplessness often, in hunger and thirst, in fasting often, in cold and nakedness* (2 Corinthians 11:24-27).

His perseverance and strength is to be admired, for many of us would be inclined to become depressed during trials and tribulations, especially if we are serving God as vehemently and audaciously as Paul served Him throughout his life. But when we know God as Paul knew Him, we can lift Him up no matter what we are experiencing in our lives.

In chapter 1 of Philippians, Paul explains to the believers that they shouldn't despair over his imprisonment because what has happened to him is helping spread the Gospel, and his experiences in prison are stimulating and encouraging other believers to willingly take a stand for Christ and preach the Gospel, regardless of the consequences. He says,

> *But I want you to know, brethren, that the things which happened to me have actually turned out for the furtherance of the gospel, so that it has become evident to the whole palace guard, and to all the rest, that my chains are in Christ; and most of the brethren in the Lord, having become confident by my chains, are much more bold to speak the word without fear* (Philippians 1:12-14).

Essentially, he is telling us that when we have the mind of Christ, we can face anything simply because of the strength of our minds. Why? Paul knew that as long as his mind was connected to Christ, he would be able to overcome all trials and tribulations.

Every believer needs to see God from a position of *"I AM always enough."* We need to know that the Most High God is saying to each and every one of us:

- I AM enough when you have nothing.

- I AM enough to heal you.

- I AM enough to deliver you.

- I AM enough when everyone is against you.

- I AM enough when you don't have money.

* I AM enough for whatever you need.

Paul is actually saying, "My life is not my own; it belongs to Christ. If I die, I will be out of this body and with the Lord." Without a doubt, we are to mirror Paul's attitude by saying, "What can you do worse to me than take my life? If I am not afraid to die, then surely I will rejoice and enjoy my life." Paul understood the value of knowing that God is sufficient. He said, *"We are confident, yes well pleased rather to be absent from the body and be present with the Lord"* (2 Cor. 5:8).

The apostle Paul was not the kind of guy to hang out with if you didn't have the same commitment that he possessed. Just think how you would feel if you were locked in a cell with Paul in a Roman prison and you want him to be quiet, but he wants to keep talking about Jesus. At the same time, you know that Nero is killing Christians and feeding them to the lions. To this day, you can still visit the great coliseum in Rome where Christians were burned and devoured by lions for entertainment at sports events. If you were cell mates with Paul when he was talking about Christ Jesus, you might want to say, "It's all right to pray quietly, Paul, but let's not have any big discussions about how living is Christ and dying is gain." But Paul had no problem saying just that—*"For me to live is Christ, and to die is gain"* (Phil. 1:21). Paul's attitude was, "I don't care what Caesar is doing; I don't care what the emperor is doing; I am going to enjoy my God."

Every child of God should be able to say, "If God brought me from the dead once, then the devil can't scare me with the threat of dying." If you came out of the trenches once, satan can't tell you when or how you should praise your God. It is far better to have the devil angry because you are praising God, then for you not to praise God in order to keep the devil happy. If the devil is chasing you, you can run into God's arms; but where do you go if God is coming after you? Your circumstances should never dictate the quality of our relationship with God; you are to praise God at all times. Psalm 34:1 says, *"I will bless the Lord at all times; His praise shall continually be in my mouth."* Your circumstances should never dictate the quality of your praise and relationship with God.

When you compare your situations or circumstances to the mountains and valleys that others are experiencing, you may discover that your biggest problem is very small. There are some people—no matter how low they sink in the valley of sickness, pain, suffering, persecutions, and tribulations—who are still able to experience more joy than others who may be living at the highest pinnacle of fame and fortune in their lives.

The conclusion is that no matter how far one person climbs on the highest mountain or how low another person falls to the deepest valley of pain and suffering, neither circumstance will determine how much each person will praise the Lord.

As Christian believers, we ought to be so high in our praises that even when we are at the lowest point in our lives, we can still find enough strength and faith to say, *"I will bless the Lord at all times; His praise shall continually be in my mouth"* (Ps. 34:1). As we encourage someone else and say, "In the name of Jesus, come on up a little higher," we can also say, as Peter said, *"Silver and gold, have I none, but such as I have I give thee; in the name of Jesus Christ of Nazareth, rise up and walk"* (Acts 3:6 KJV).

# PART THREE

# A NEW MIND

The first key to freedom is acquiring a new mind. Paul told the Roman church that transformation was dependent upon obtaining a renewed mind. Your thinking determines your actions. Negative thinking will enslave you and steal your freedom.

Because the old mind has been corrupted by sin, negativity, and rejection, it doesn't need just a little change here and there; it needs a total overhaul. Getting a new mind is a process. Once you begin to experience this new way of thinking, you will begin to enjoy a new way of living.

## CHAPTER ELEVEN

# ACHIEVING UNITY THROUGH HUMILITY

## PAUL'S MESSAGE—HAVING THE SAME MIND

In chapter 2 of Philippians, Paul presents a case for unity to the people of the church in Philippi. Paul declares that in order to gain unity, there must be humility. He deals with the concept of humility in verse 5 after he argumentatively suggests in verse 1 that there is consolation in Christ: *"If there be therefore any consolation in Christ, if any comfort of love, if any fellowship of the Spirit, if any bowels and mercies"* (Phil. 2:1 KJV). While each *if* (Greek: *ei*) seems to be a subjunctive, it is not; *ie*, the word for "if" in the Greek concept, is actually declaring a condition that exists. Thus, each *if* in Philippians 2:1 should be translated as "because." Verse 1 would then read, "Because there is consolation in Christ, because there is comfort of love, because we have fellowship of the Spirit, because there are affections of mercy." Paul is actually saying, "As Christians, we have appeal in our union with Christ Jesus because *we have* consolation in Christ, *we have* comfort of love, *we have* fellowship of the Spirit, and *we have* affection of mercies.

Paul dearly loved and appreciated the Philippians, and he shared great joy with them. So he now brings the church from rejoicing to the idea of exaltation and unity. He begins with, *"Fulfill my joy"* (Greek: *chara*) by being *"greatly and exceedingly joyful."* He feels that he will have even more joy and that his joy will be made full or complete if all the members are working together in unity and love by being like-minded. In looking at the word *like-minded* in Greek, we find that this word, *isopsuchos*, literally means "of equal soul." It comes from two words—*isos*, meaning "equal," and *psuche*, meaning "the soul." Another Greek word expressing the concept of "like-minded," *homophron*, is taken from the words *homo*, "the same," and *phren*, "the mind," or think the same thing. It means, "thinking the same thing" (present tense—continuously thinking of having the same love and unity of affection).' Thus, we are to love the same things, love the Lord, and have the same love for one another. When he says, *"being of one accord* [Greek: *sumpsuchos*], *with united spirits,"* he is asking for unity of sentiment and for the members to think and act as if they are but one soul, one mind.

Scripture shows that the apostle Paul asked for unity at other churches as well. To the church at Corinth he writes,

> *Now I plead with you, brethren, by the name of our Lord Jesus Christ, that you speak the same thing, and that there be no divisions among you, but that you be perfectly joined together in the same mind and in the same judgment* (1 Corinthians 1:10).

In the letter to the Romans he writes,

> *Now, may the God of patience and comfort grant you to be like-minded toward one another according to Christ Jesus, that you may with one mind, and one mouth, glorify the God and Father of our Lord Jesus Christ* (Romans 15:5-6).

God is also appealing for unity in the Church today. It will bring great joy when the members are thinking the same thoughts—to love one another, to be like-minded, having the same love, and being of one accord. We are not to let petty quarrels and dissensions bring division among the members.

In essence, Paul's request is that we must be of one mind and equal soul as we seek to maintain unity with each other. It is through the love of Jesus Christ that our souls are united, our hearts are in unison, and we can truly live together in love as though we have one mind and one spirit between us.

Paul takes us to another level of thinking when he introduces the concept of humility in verse 3 of Philippians 2. He instructs that we are to humble ourselves, let go of our own pride, and turn away from selfish ambition or conceited attitudes in order to consider the needs of others. He admonishes that we are not to seek personal aggrandizement, but to esteem others as being more important and more worthy than oneself. We are family in the Lord, sharing the same Holy Spirit, and our hearts are to be tender and sympathetic at all times.

## A HUMBLE MIND

Plato and other philosophers have inquired whether humility is a virtue, but virtue or not, they have agreed that nothing is more rare than lowliness of mind. The Greeks called it *tapeinosis* or *tapeineia*—"lowliness of mind."

- Plato strongly recommended in the fourth book of the *Laws* of Plato, where he rejects the proud and would multiply the humble.[2]

- John Calvin maintains, "All the blessings we enjoy are Divine deposits, committed to our trust on this condition, that they should be dispensed for the benefit of our neighbors."[3]

- John Locke says, "To love our neighbor as ourselves is such a truth of regulating human society, that by that alone one might determine all the cases in social morality."[4]

It is from both theology and philosophy that we are admonished to work together as a Church to fulfill the commission that God has given us—to love one another and to "be of humble mind, laying aside all haughtiness, and pride, and foolishness, and angry feelings...being especially mindful of the words of the Lord Jesus which He spoke, teaching us meekness and long-suffering."[5]

When we look at what's happening in churches today, we find that some people have been alienated from church because it has become a battleground of conflict that has nothing to do with the Gospel. Most conflicts among Christians are rooted in self-centeredness—fights and quarrels caused, not by some external source, but by the people's evil desires. Disagreements often come about because members, deacons, elders, and sometimes even pastors, seek positions of power and status. Consequently, when everyone seeks his or her own pleasure, only strife and hatred result.

Selfish ambition leads to division and strife and thus creates different moods, different spirits, and different attitudes throughout the sanctuary.

In addressing conflicts among the members, the Bible says:

> *Where do wars and fights come from among you? Do they not come from your desires for pleasure that war in your members? ...Or do you think that the Scripture says in vain the Spirit who dwells in us yearns jealously? But He gives grace. Therefore He says; "God resists the proud, but gives grace to the humble"* (James 4:1,5-6).

James calls for believers to humble themselves. True faith is humility. And humility is the opposite of the proud selfishness and self-centered ambition that characterizes this present evil age. When disagreements occur in the church, you are to be wise enough to understand how to handle them correctly with godly wisdom.

The Word is clear—pride promotes strife, but humility can cure worldliness. Humility must be expressed in order to gain unity. And in order to have unity, you must be willing to offer yourself to meet the needs of others. For example, if participants in the music ministry want to sing melodiously and uniformly, they must attend rehearsals. The members must give up something and make adjustments to their lives and schedules in order to dedicate themselves to the rehearsals. If, however, the music ministers adopt the attitude, "I will go to rehearsal only when it is convenient for me," they will never have a unified voice. Why? When people act as individuals in a collective environment, it creates problems, defeating teamwork and effective group participation. The individual members will have to humble themselves for the benefit of the group.

In essence, you must cultivate a spirit of Christian humility and regard others as more important than yourself. Paul admonishes that you must not only be concerned about your interests, but you must be concerned about the interests of others. He maintains that you need to do the right thing even when you think no one is looking. He says, *"Therefore, my beloved, as you have always obeyed, not as in my presence only, but now much more in my absence, work out your own salvation with fear and trembling"*

(Phil. 2:12). You must love the people who come into the church because it is the right thing to do; you must humble yourself and treat others with love and dignity because the consolation you have in Christ is an incentive and motivation for unity in the Holy Spirit.

## OUR COMMON BOND IS JESUS

Paul advises that the Holy Spirit, the power of God, will move more vigorously in the Church if there is fellowship of the Spirit. When there is fellowship of the Spirit, there is joint participation among all the members in things that are common to each other. Fellowship of the Spirit causes the members to be like-minded, have the same love, be of one accord, and be of one mind so that there can be joint participation in things that are common to each other. When he says, *"this joint participation in things that are common to each other,"* he is giving us the definition of *fellowship* (Greek: *koinonia*), which is, sharing in unity or shared by all. In order for there to be fellowship and joint participation, there must be agreement on a common or central purpose, and the one thing that is common among believers in the Church is *Jesus*.

When we come together and call on the name of Jesus, it does not matter if one person eloquently describes Him and another person says His name in a simple dialect; as long as we are together as one and keep our minds on the Lord Jesus, the devil can't break up the house of God. Likewise, when the storms of life begin to rage in our homes and personal situations, we are to assemble our mates, children, and family members together to touch and agree in the name of Jesus. The devil cannot move against the house and family who focuses on the Lord because *"where two or three are gathered together in My name, I am there in the midst of them"* (Matt. 18:20).

Because it is God's desire for love and harmony to permeate the church congregation, we must live unselfishly and turn away from selfish ambitions or conceited attitudes. We must maintain unity with other believers in our thoughts, attitudes, love, spirit, and purpose. And where there is unity, the members of the church will have one thing in common—the Lord Jesus as Savior and the devil as the enemy.

Paul says there are some among the believers who are not controlled by the Holy Spirit. Hence, when the Lord moves through the Church, we don't recognize Him because we are not focused on Him. But God says, "If I can get two or three to touch and agree (focus on Me), I will be in their midst." The Holy Spirit will let the devil know that he cannot claim this territory because the members' minds are stayed on Christ Jesus. Jesus is the star in the household of faith, and when Jesus is the star, the Holy Spirit will destroy everything the devil is attempting to do.

The question now becomes: If each saint is indwelled by the Holy Spirit, why is there not unity among the saints? The answer is clear: It's not by virtue of the indwelling of the Holy Spirit; it's by virtue of His control of your life. Yes, you can be indwelled by the Holy Spirit a long time before the Spirit has control of you, and there is a difference. In many circumstances people can struggle to achieve a higher height in God, yet the Spirit of God has no control in their lives. And so, the Church can be easily infiltrated with rifts and divisions, and where there are rifts and divisions, the doors are opened for warring, fighting, and contentious attitudes.

When the Spirit of Christ is in control of our lives, we are able to work out the struggles and disagreements because the Holy Spirit directs us, guides us, and leads us through what is significant in our lives. The Holy Spirit has a way of removing insignificant matters from our minds and wills; then He causes us to fellowship with people who have a common purpose. In other words, when we come to kneel together, to pray together, to praise together, and to worship together, we have one thing in common—Christ Jesus is our Savior, who provides an example of a sacrificial and humble mind, and the devil is our enemy.

# CHAPTER TWELVE

# EXCHANGING YOUR MIND FOR GOD'S MIND

Paul presents Jesus as a perfect example of unselfishness and instructs, *"Let this mind be in you which was also in Christ Jesus"* (Phil. 2:5). Jesus Christ is our example of the sacrificial mind, the serving mind, the humble mind, and the mind of love. When we have the mind of Christ, we have the indwelling of the Holy Spirit, the indwelling of the Father and the Son in our transformed and renewed minds. And with the mind of Christ, we should be willing to adopt Christ's attitude of love, unselfishness, servant-hood, humility, and obedience, looking beyond our own interests for the sake of others.

Humility is not a problem when we love. Most of us humble ourselves from time to time—usually to the ones we love. For example, two ladies lived next door to each other for many years. One lady rose at three o'clock in the morning and looked through the window and saw that her neighbor was in the kitchen. Later that day she asked, "What were you doing up at three o'clock this morning?"

The neighbor responded, "I was cooking for my husband; he had just gotten home."

"You got up at three to cook for your husband?" the nosey neighbor asked and continued, "I would never get up at three o'clock to cook for anybody."

The wife then responded, "I love my husband, and I will get up at any time to cook for him."

When love is in place, getting up at three o'clock in the morning is not much of a sacrifice. You have to be mindful that listening to other people who want to tell you what you should or should not do; it can destroy your relationship and fellowship with the ones you love.

Love has even caused parents to mortgage their homes for a child, even when they believed that the child had committed a crime. Whenever there is love, you will bless somebody with whatever you have, and you will lower yourself to pick someone else up. When God blesses you with someone special, you are to humble yourself to develop and strengthen loving relationships and fellowship through the Holy Spirit. Serving someone else doesn't make you less of a person; it actually makes you better.

Remember, when you humble yourself, the Lord will raise you up (see James 4:10). And when God raises you up, He gives you blessings so that you may have life and have it more abundantly (see John 10:10). So as Christians, we are to treat one another with the same spirit as we experience in Christ Jesus and have the same attitude as our Lord and Savior.

## JESUS—IN THE FORM OF GOD

Paul takes us from having the mind of Christ to the nature and essence of Christ. Philippians 2:6 says, *"Who being in the form of God...."* The words *"form of God"* (Greek: *morphe Theou*) refer to God's divine nature. The divine nature cannot be separated from the person of Christ because His nature and essence are Deity. What this means is that Jesus Christ possesses and expresses all of God's attributes because He is God. While Jesus was in the form of God, He was fully God, and He was fully man. E.H. Gifford concludes, "The Son of God could not possibly divest Himself of the form of God at His incarnation without thereby ceasing to be God."[1]

Paul continues in verse 8 with one of the most important passages on Christology—the *kenosis* or "Christ self-emptying." Scripture shows that Christ Jesus laid aside the independent use of His divine attributes for a time. *"And being found in appearance as a man, He humbled Himself and became obedient to the point of death, even the death of the cross"* (Phil. 2:8). Christ Jesus divested Himself of His Deity, but withheld His pre-incarnate glory, and He voluntarily restricted His use of certain attributes (for example, omnipresence and omniscience). This is a consummate picture of Jesus Christ as we truly understand the all-sufficiency of Christ, His incarnation, and His crucifixion (see Phil. 2:5-11).

It's imperative to note that when we look at the word *form,* our minds immediately consider pulchritude or shape because, to us, a form is something of structure, which has definite boundaries and borders. Actually, it speaks of the shape or external appearance of a body without the essential qualities. It is the outside appearance and not what is on the inside. It may even *"have a form of godliness, but* [be] *denying its power..."* (2 Tim. 3:5). But God is an omnipresent Spirit, and a spirit has no shape.

So Paul is not talking about the physical shape of Christ, but of His divine essence. He is talking about a philosophical expression *form,* which is an outward expression of an inward essence or character. When he says, *"Jesus was in the form of God,"* the word *form* is an expression of *being,* which carries in itself the distinctive nature and characteristic of Christ as the expression of God. Jesus is the image of the invisible God—not another god or a part of a god. Jesus Christ is the God of the Old Testament robed in flesh. The Bible tells us, *"In the beginning was the Word, and the Word was with God, and the Word was God...and the Word became flesh and dwelt among us..."* (John 1:1,14). The Word was with God in the beginning and actually was God Himself.

It must be made crystal clear—Christ Jesus was truly one with the Father, in glory equal, majesty co-eternal. Yet He made Himself of no reputation. Jesus, in a pristine state with angels flying around Him at all levels, did something remarkable. He changed that outward expression and took on the "form of a servant" (Greek: *morphe doulos*). Christ Jesus with His majestic, magnanimous beauty took on the form of a servant. He gave up the manifestation of Deity and assumed real humanity. In other words, He emptied Himself of Himself—of that divine fullness—and He willingly relinquished the glory He had with the Father before the world began. Then Jesus took out the godliness and put on the form of a servant.

We must clearly understand that Deity was always a part of Jesus Christ, and the use of the word *form* refers to a preexisting state. It did not change when He took on the form of a man. *Matthew Henry's Commentary* says, "Christ not only took upon Him the likeness and fashion, or form of a man, but of one in a low state; not appearing in splendor."[2]

He became flesh and voluntarily emptied Himself and went from glory in Heaven to the profound depths of hell. It was because of love that Christ Jesus consummated His sinless obedience to the will of God by becoming obedient to the point of death, even death on a cross.

The incarnation existed in the mind of God before the world began. Scripture records, *"He indeed was foreordained before the foundation of the world, but was manifest in these last times for you"* (1 Pet. 1:20). It is significant to note that Hegel regarded Christianity as the highest form of religion. He said, "For in Christianity, the truth that the Absolute manifests itself in the finite is symbolically reflected in the incarnation."[3]

Even though Jesus was in the form of God, expressing God, He thought it not robbery to be equal with God, because He was God. When Paul says in Philippians 2:6, *"did not consider it robbery,"* we find that there are several meanings for this word *robbery*—one is "a thing unlawfully seized"; to rob something is to take it by force. Because Jesus Christ has the form of God, He didn't walk into Heaven to take the form of God from God. We, therefore, conclude that He has to be God.

The second meaning is a "treasure to be clutched or retained," no matter how dangerous the circumstances are. Again, we must conclude that we can't steal the form of God from God; you can't rob God. So to be equal with God in this expression is to possess God. Jesus is the expression and nature of God.

## HUMILITY AND LOVE

When you combine humility with love, you forget your ego and do what God requires of you. You say to others, "I am here to help you develop to your fullest potential so that God can receive the glory from your life as well as from my life." So with love and humility you can say, "It is not about me." Remember, when you humble yourself, the Lord shall raise you up. And when God raises you up, He gives you blessings so you *"may have life and...have it more abundantly"* (John 10:10).

Thus, being equal with God refers to the mode of Jesus Christ's existence. He willingly relinquished His glory when He came to earth, though retaining His Deity. This is now Deity having an expression, not a shape, because God is everywhere. Everywhere is formless from the point of view of shape, and everywhere is the expression of God. So far, there is no English word that can convey the word *form* any differently. It's not even possible to formulate the reality of this expression that comes from God. All we know is that, philosophically, God has an expression of who He is, and Jesus Christ is the expression of God.

Let's assume that all the celestial creatures, even though they don't know God's shape, understand His expression. Christ Jesus expresses God through His innate character and nature. It's the mode of the expression that is the setting of divine essence, but it is not identical with the essence itself. In other words, there is the essence, which is God (Deity), and God has an expression, which is Jesus Christ (the form of the expression). In order to have Jesus Christ (the form), you have to have the God (the Deity), but Jesus Christ (the form) is not identical with God (the Deity), even though Jesus Christ is an equal expression of God.

When we take this a little deeper, we can compare form, as if we are dealing with light from fire. The light from the fire is not the fire. As we get close to the fire, we feel the warmth, but the warmth is not the fire. The fire is giving off the expression of heat and light; but the fire is more than the expression even though the expression of heat and light are true replica of the essence of the fire. There is more to the fire than heat. There is more to the fire than light. So when talking about the form, the form and the expression are not the true essence of who Christ really is. There is more to Christ Jesus than His form and expression—Jesus Christ is Lord. Because no one can walk up to God and rob Him of His form and expression, He has to really be in the form of God to express God—"...*Jesus Christ is Lord...*" (Phil. 2:11).

Can you imagine God in His pristine holiness, in His celestial environment with angels, cherubim, and seraphim worshiping Him? Even the spiritual creatures who don't love God have to respect Him. They have to respect Him because He is God. The following scenario may help you to grasp the meaning that God is supreme and only God can be God.

In the Book of Daniel, as Daniel prayed, an angel was sent from Heaven with an answer. The Bible says that the prince of Persia, who is another angel, stopped the angel coming from God. The prince of Persia stopped the angel from Heaven in his tracks for 21 days; consequently, the angel from Heaven couldn't get through to Daniel. How did he eventually get free? Michael the archangel commanded the prince of Persia to release the angel that was sent from Heaven.

When the angel with the message from God finally got through and opened his mouth, the Scripture says it sounded like a multitude. Can you imagine one voice sounding like a stadium of people at a football game? The Bible says that right away, Daniel's strength left him and he fell down. (See Daniel 10:8-15.)

Notice that these angels can be placed on a scale by ranked order. The angel from Heaven (first rank) had a voice like all of us together. The prince of Persia (second rank) stopped the angel from Heaven. Michael the archangel (third rank) stopped the prince of Persia. But when Michael was looking at the devil (fourth rank), the Bible says, he dared not make an accusation against satan. Michael the archangel said, *"The Lord* [top rank—all power] *rebukes you"* (Jude 9).

If Michael is this powerful, can you imagine the power of God? Jesus was in the form of God. And Jesus in the form of God was in the mode of expression that set the divine essence of who He was. Thus, the expression is not the same as the essence, because Jesus is the expression of the essential nature that shows Jesus is God.

## BALANCING DEITY AND HUMANITY

Because Christ Jesus willingly laid aside His heavenly glory to come to earth and die, you should be willing to adopt Christ's attitude of love, unselfishness, servanthood, humility, and obedience, looking beyond your own interest for the sake of others.

We now know that Jesus was and is God and that He went from the infinite heights of a pristine glory in Heaven to the infinite profound depths of hell. He was the Word of God who became flesh and lived among people for 33 years; He was obedient to death. The Bible tells us that:

- Christ existed in the form of God.

- He was with God.

- He was equal to God.

- He became flesh.

- Even though He was Deity, He was truly human.

- As a man, He became a servant to God and humanity.

- He was obedient to God the Father.

- He lived a perfectly sinless life, which qualified Him to step into our place to receive the wrath of God toward sin.

- His death provided the necessary basis for redemption.

Again, we must recognize the word *form* (*morphe*). He came in the form of a servant, being made in the likeness of a man. But although Jesus was in the likeness of a man, He was more than a man. His humanity was genuine, yet He was still divine. The Bible declares that the fullness of God was in Jesus from the moment of His incarnation—from the moment His human life began. Scripture clearly and unequivocally shows Jesus as God in the flesh. Prior to His incarnation, Jesus was in the form of God and existed as essentially equal and one with God (see John 1:1-3).

As Lord and Savior, Jesus could have considered holding on to His godliness. He could have held on to the cherubim and seraphim and all of the other things around Him. Jesus could have looked to the earth, saw humankind living in sin, and said, "I am God, and I am not going to change." But when He saw us covered in sin, He refused to hold on to His godliness and let us die in our sin.

Christ shared in the glories and prerogatives of Deity, but did not regard the circumstances of His existence as something to be jealously retained. Rather, He willingly relinquished His glory when He came to earth. When Jesus took on a human form, He humbled Himself to accomplish that task for which He had come—to die for sinful humanity in order that we might have eternal life. Jesus loved you so much that He humbled and emptied Himself of His glory and became flesh to save humankind.

## CHAPTER THIRTEEN

# ACHIEVING PRISTINE FOR THE MUNDANE

What exactly did Jesus give up when He came to earth? He gave up the expression, but He did not give up His godliness.

- He did not give up His omniscience; He is God.
- He did not give up His omnipresence; He is God.
- He did not give up His immutability; He is God.
- He did not give up His omnipotence; He is God.

Scripture says,

> *He has no form or comeliness; and when we see Him, there was no beauty that we should desire Him. He is despised and rejected by men, a Man of sorrows and acquainted with grief...He was despised and we did not esteemed Him* (Isaiah 53:2b-3).

The Son of man came not to be ministered unto, but to minister and to save (see Matt. 20:28). He renounced the glory of Heaven to suffer and die for our salvation. Indeed, what did He give up?

- He gave up the pristine—His glory—for the mundane—our sins.
- He came and subjected Himself to nine months in a woman's womb as He wrapped Himself up in panoply of flesh. He

131

held her up while she carried Him (see Luke 1:31; Matt. 1:23; Isa. 7:14).

- He owned cattle on a thousand hills, but was born in a manger (see Luke 2:7).

- He subjected Himself to hunger even while He created all the food (see Matt. 21:18; Luke 4:2).

- He subjected Himself to exhaustion while He was the energy of the world (see John 4:6).

- He subjected Himself to being questioned when He was above any question that anyone could ask (see Matt. 27:12-14; Mark 14:3-4; Luke 23:9; John 19:9).

- He subjected Himself to being ignored even though He had the power to cut off all oxygen.

- He subjected Himself to being ridiculed (see Matt. 9:24).

- He was spat on and cursed. They mocked Him, but He kept the servant form (see Matt. 26:67).

- They dragged Him through three courts and crushed a crown of thorns upon His head. They flogged Him with a flagdrum and hung Him on a cross. Still, He was God (see Mark 15:16-20).

- He gave His life. He died on the Cross and was buried in a tomb.

But three days later, He rose from the grave with all power in His hands. God exalted Christ Jesus to the highest place, and He made a name for Himself.

*Therefore Gid also has highly exalted Him and gave Him the name which is above every name, that at the name of Jesus, every knee should bow, of those in heaven, and of those on earth, and of those under the earth, and that every tongue should confess that Jesus Christ is Lord, to the glory of God the Father* (Philippians 2:9-11).

## CHAPTER FOURTEEN

# EXALTED TO THE HIGHEST PLACE

After Jesus Christ was raised from the dead, God the Father restored to Him the glory that He had before His humiliation and exalted Him to the highest place—the right hand of God the Father (see John 17:5,24; Acts 2:33; 5:31; Eph. 1:20-21). After Jesus Christ descended to the lowest depth of humiliation, God exalted Him to the highest place in eternity. God the Father also conferred on Him the name that is supreme above every name.

The Lord Jesus Christ is the name that is above every name. The name *Lord* [Greek: *kurios*] is the Old Testament name for God. The supreme name is translated to the divine name *Yahweh*. This title of "Lord" places Him in the position of Sovereign Ruler over all things. His power and authority encompasses every age and exceeds every known power, now and in the future.

The name of Jesus Christ is far above all principality and power and might and dominion and every name that is named, not only in this age, but also in that which is to come (see Eph. 1:20-22). There are many names used in reference to Jesus Christ; common names we often use are:

- Jehovah-Rohi, my shepherd
- Jehovah-Nissi, my banner
- Jehovah-MKaddesh, sanctifies me
- Jehovah-Shalom, my peace
- Jehovah-Tsidkenu, my righteousness
- Jehovah-Rophe, my healer

These are limited names in limited circumstances, but there is a name that is above every name. You know the name. It's the name of Jesus. Jesus—that's the name. That's the name we use when we ask:

- Who is this with power from on high?
- Who is this with healing in His hand?
- Who is this who can make day out of night?
- Who is this who can talk to a drug addict while he is high?
- Who is this who can take AIDS out of your blood?
- Who is this who can set you free from all kinds of sickness?

## THE NAME ABOVE EVERY NAME

Because the name of Jesus is exalted over and above all creation, all things in Heaven, in earth, and under the earth will bow down and confess that Jesus is Lord. Every man, woman, and child is under the authority and rule of Jesus Christ. Even those who refuse to bend the knee to acknowledge through confession will one day acknowledge and confess that Jesus is Lord. At the name of Jesus, every knee will bow—high and low, good and bad, saved and unsaved, including satan and all his demons. *"And that every tongue shall confess that Jesus Christ is Lord, to the glory of God the Father"* (Phil. 2:11).

## CHAPTER FIFTEEN

# THEOLOGICAL AND PHILOSOPHICAL THOUGHTS AND CONCEPTS

| THE POWER OF A HUMBLE MIND IS A MIND OF LOVE | |
|---|---|
| THEOLOGY | PHILOSOPHY |
| As Christ Jesus gave up His heavenly glory to come to earth in the form of a man and suffer death on the cross, we should be willing to adopt Christ's attitude of unselfishness, servanthood, humility, and obedience; and look beyond our own interest for the sake of others. | Philosophers have enquired whether humility is a virtue; but virtue or not, everyone must agree that nothing is more rare. The Greeks called it tapeinosis or tapeineia—"lowliness of mind." It is strongly recommended in the fourth book of the Laws of Plato: he rejects the proud and would multiply the humble.[1] |
| Philippians 2:3-4—*"Do nothing from selfishness or empty conceit, but with humility of mind regard one another as more important than yourselves; do not merely look out for your own personal interests, but also for the interests of others"* (NASB) | John Calvin—"All the blessings we enjoy are Divine deposits, committed to our trust on this condition, that they should be dispensed for the benefit of our neighbors."[2] |
| Philippians 2:5—*"Have this attitude in yourselves which was also in Christ Jesus"* (NASB) | John Locke—"To love our neighbor as ourselves is such a truth of regulating human society, that by that alone one might determine all the cases in social morality."[3] |
| Galatians 5:26—*"Let us not become boastful, challenging one another, envying one another"* (NASB) | |

| THE POWER OF A HUMBLE MIND IS A MIND OF LOVE | |
|---|---|
| **THEOLOGY** | **PHILOSOPHY** |
| Romans 12:3—*"For I say, through the grace given to me, to everyone who is among you, not to think of himself more highly than he ought to think, but to think soberly, as God has dealt to each one a measure of faith."*<br><br>Romans 12:10—*"Be kindly affectionate to one another giving preference to one another."* | Saint Augustine—"What does love look like? It has the hands to help oth- ers. It has the feet to hasten to the poor and needy. It has eyes to see misery and want. It has the ears to hear the sighs and sorrows of men. That is what love looks like."[4]<br><br>Aristotle—"We become just by per- forming just action, temperate by per- for ming temperate things, brave by performing brave action."[5]<br><br>Albert Einstein—"My religion consists of a humble admiration of the illim- itable superior spirit who reveals him- self in the slight details we to perceive with out frail and feeble mind."[6] |

# MEANINGS AND EXPLANATIONS WITH USE AND APPLICATION

## EMPTIED (Greek: kenoo\ken-o-o),

*Emptied Himself (Greek: eauton kenoo, sen)*

**Strong's Concordance #2758:** to make empty, i.e. to abase, neutralize, falsify; make (of no effect, of no reputation, void), be in vain.

**Vine's Expository Dictionary:** "to empty," is so translated in Philippians. 2:7, "made...of no reputation." The clauses which follow the verb are exegetical of its meaning, especially the phrases "the form of a servant," and "the likeness of men." Christ did not "empty" Himself of Godhood. He did not cease to be what He essentially and eternally was.

**Webster' Dictionary:** unoccupied; containing nothing; lacking reality, substance, meaning, or value; devoid of sense; marked by the absence of human life; and to remove the contents.

**Use and Application:** Jesus Christ became flesh and voluntarily "emptied" (to pour out) Himself and went from glory in Heaven to the profound depths of hell.

## EXISTED (Greek: huparcho\hoop-ar-kho)

**Strong's Concordance #5225:** from *hupo* (under), to begin under (quietly), i.e. come into existence (be present at hand); expletively to exist—after behave, live.

**Vine's Expository Dictionary:** Primarily, "to make a beginning" (*hupo*, "under," *arche*, "a beginning"), denotes "to be, to be in existence," involving an "existence" or condition both previous to the circumstances mentioned and continuing after it. This is important in Philippians 2:6 concerning the deity of Christ.

**Webster's Dictionary:** To come into being, to stand, stop; to have a real being whether material or spiritual; to have being in a specified place or with respect to understood limitations or conditions.

**Use and Application:** The phrase "being (existing) in the form (*morphe*, the essential and specific form and character) of God," carries with it the two facts of the antecedent Godhood of Christ, previous to His incarnation, and the continuance of His Godhood at and after the event of His birth.

## FELLOWSHIP (Greek: koinonia\Koy-nohn-ee'-ah)

**Strong's Concordance #2842:** partnership, i.e. participation, or social intercourse, or (pecuniary) benefaction: communicate, communion, distribution, fellowship.

**Vine's Expository Dictionary:** communion, fellowship, sharing in common.

**Webster's Dictionary:** to join in fellowship with a church member; to admit to fellowship (as in church).

**Use and Application:** In *koionia* the individual shares in common an intimate bond of fellowship and shared in communion of Christ and the Body of Christ, as set forth by the emblems in the Lord's Supper. Fellowship (*koinonia*) cements the believers to the Lord Jesus and to each other.

## FORM (Greek: Morphe\mor-fay),

*Form of God (Greek: en morphe Theou)*

**Strong's Concordance #3444:** refers to form (through the idea of adjustment of parts); shape; nature; form.

**Vine's Expository Dictionary:** Denotes "the special characteristic form or feature" of a person or thing; it is used with particular significance in the New Testament, only of Christ in Philippians 2:6,7, in the phrase "being in the form of God," and "taking the form of a servant." An excellent definition of the word is that of Gifford: *morphe* is the essence form which never alters;

not in the abstract, but as actually subsisting in the individual, and retained as long as the individual itself exists....Thus, *morphe Theou* is the Divine nature actually and inseparably subsisting in the Person of Christ....For the interpretation of "the form of God" it is sufficient to say that He partakes all the essential attributes of deity. It includes the whole nature and essence of Deity, and is inseparable from them, since they could have no actual existence without it. The true meaning of *morphe* in the expression "form of God" is confirmed by its recurrence in the corresponding phrase, "form of a servant." It is universally admitted that the two phrases are directly antithetical, and that *form* must, therefore, have the same sense in both.

**Webster's Dictionary:** To give a particular shape; to shape or mold into a certain state or after a particular model.

**Use and Application:** Existing as He already did in the form of God, Christ Jesus was an expression of God's divine nature and attributes because He was fully God.

## GRASPED (Greek: harpagmos\har-pag-mos)

*Did not regard equality with God a thing to be grasped (Greek: Ouch harpagmon hegesato to einai isa theo)*

**Strong's Concordance #725:** plunder—robbery, to seize, pluck, pull, take (by force).

**Vine's Expository Dictionary:** "to seize, carry off by force," is found in Philippians 2:6, "(counted it not) a prize, "a thing to be grasped." *To be grasped"* (*Harpagmos* is from a Greek word which has two meanings, "a thing unlawfully seized," and "a prize or treasure to be retained at all hazards": (1) in the active sense, the act of seizing, robbery; (2) in the passive sense, a thing held as a prize. *"Grasped"* originally meant *"a thing seized by robbery"* and eventually came to mean anything clutched, embraced, or prized, thus is sometimes translated "grasped" or "held onto." A treasure to be clutched and retained.

**Webster's Dictionary:** To seize with or as if with a grapple; come to grips with; wrestle to bind closely.

**Use and Application:** Christ Jesus did not regard equality with God as a "*harpagmos*"—something to be grasped, snatched, or seized as a robber.

He did not have to retain by force His equality with God. He did not regard His being on an equality of glory and majesty with God as a prize and a treasure to be held fast, but He emptied Himself thereof.

## HIGHLY EXALTED
### (Greek: Huperupsoo\hoop-er-oop-sah-oh)

**Strong's Concordance #5251:** to elevate above others, i.e. raise to the highest position: highly exalt.

**Vine's Expository Dictionary:** To exalt highly; is used of Christ, as in Philippians 2:9.

**Webster's Dictionary:** To raise in rank, power, or character; to elevate by praise or in estimation and glorify.

**Use and Application:** This means "to raise to supreme majesty"; it refers to a super-eminent exaltation. Thus, the word suggests exaltation to the highest position, an elevation above all others. The context contrasts humiliation and resulting honors. Jesus' obedience to death is followed by a super-exalted position of honor and glory.

## HUMBLED
### (Greek: tapeinoo\ta-pa-no-o)

*He humbled himself (Greek: heauton tapeinoo)*

**Strong's Concordance #5013:** To depress; to humiliate (in condition or heart; abase, bring low, humble self.

**Vine's Expository Dictionary:** Signifies to make low; to be abased.

**Webster's Dictionary:** not proud or haughty; not arrogant or assertive; reflecting, expressing, or offered in a spirit of pretense and deception.

**Use and Application:** To describe a person who is devoid of all arrogance and self-exaltation—a person who is willingly submitted to God and His will.

## HUMILITY (lowliness of mind)
### (Greek: tapeinophrosune\ tap-i-nof-ros-oo-nay)

**Strong's Concordance #5012:** The base of humiliation of mind, i.e. modesty; humbleness of mind, humility, lowliness of mind.

**Vine's Expository Dictionary:** The word is a combination of *tapei-nos,* "humble," and *phren,* "mind." The lowliness of mind" (*tapeinos,* under "humble," and *phren,* "the mind"), is rendered "humility of mind."

**Webster's Dictionary:** the quality or state of being humble.

**Use and Application:** Humility is a total absence of arrogance, conceit, and haughtiness. The central thought is freedom from pride—lowliness, meekness, modesty, mildness, humble-mindedness, a sense of moral insignificance, and a humble attitude of unselfish concern for the welfare of others. Only by abstaining from self-aggrandizement can members of the Christian community maintain unity and harmony.

## INCARNATION

The word *incarnation* does not appear in the Bible. It is a theological term derived from the Latin words *in* and *caro* (flesh), and it means "to be clothed in flesh." It is the act of becoming flesh. Its only use in theology is in reference to the gracious, voluntary act of the Son of God in which He assumed a human body. Christianity teaches that the Lord Jesus Christ, the eternal Son of God, became a man who had an earthly, physical, fleshly body just like yours and mine.

There is a difference between the incarnation and the virgin birth of our Lord. The incarnation speaks of the fact of God becoming human in the person of Jesus Christ. The virgin birth, on the other hand, is the method by which God the Son became human. It is the method or means by which He took on our flesh without taking on our fallen sinful nature. By means of the virgin birth, He could remain sinless.

## LIKENESS (Greek: homoioma\hom-oy-mah)

*Likeness of men (Greek: homoioma anthropos)*

**Strong's Concordance #3667:** A form; resemblance; made like to, likeness, shape, similitude.

**Vine's Expository Dictionary:** Denotes "that which is made like something, a resemblance," "the likeness of men." From *homoioos,* similar (in appearance or character); denotes "that which is made like something, a resemblance," "(for) the likeness (of an image);" the AV translates it as a verb, "(into an image) made like to;" the association here of the two words *homoioma* and *eikon* "(the) likeness (of sinful flesh);" in Philippians 2:7 "the likeness of men." "The expression 'likeness of men' does not of itself imply, still less does it exclude or diminish, the reality of the nature which Christ assumed."

**Webster's Dictionary:** Copy, portrait, appearance, semblance, the quality or state of being like; resemblance.

**Use and Application:** Our Lord's humanity was a real likeness, not a mere phantom. But this likeness did not express the whole of Christ's nature. His mode of manifestation resembled what people are. That is declared in the words "form of a servant." Paul justly says "in the likeness of men," because, in fact, Christ, although certainly a perfect Man, was by reason of the Divine nature present in Him, not simply and merely a man, but the Incarnate Son of God.

## NAME (Greek: onoma\on'-om-ah)

*The Name which is above every name (Greek: to onoma to huper pan onoma)*

**Strong's Concordance #3686:** A "name" authority, character (called, surname).

**Vine's Expository Dictionary:** is used in general of the "name" by which a person or thing is called; in Philippians 2:9, the "Name" represents "the title and dignity" of the Lord, for all that a "name" implies, of authority, character, rank, majesty, power, excellence, etc., of everything that the "name" covers.

**Webster's Dictionary:** a word or symbol used in logic to designate an entity.

**Use and Application:** "The Name of God" in the Old Testament denotes the divine Presence, the divine Majesty, especially as the object of adoration and praise. The context here dwells on the honor and worship bestowed on Him upon whom this name was conferred. The conferring of this title, "The Name," was upon the Lord Jesus as the Son of Man.

## ROBBERY (Greek: harpagmos\har-pag-ay)

Strong's Concordance #725: plunder, robbery.

**Vine's Expository Dictionary:** "to seize, carry off by force," is found in Philippians 2:6, "(counted it not) a prize," "a thing to be grasped.", "(thought it not) robbery;" it may have two meanings, (a) in the active sense, "the act of seizing, robbery," a meaning in accordance with a rule connected with its formation; (b) in the passive sense, "a thing held as a prize," "to set forth Christ as the supreme example of humility and self-renunciation."

**Webster's Dictionary:** The act or practice of robbing; larceny from the person or presence of another by violence or threat.

**Use and Application:** "Who though He was subsisting in the essential form of God, yet did not regard His being on an equality of glory and majesty with God as a prize and a treasure to be held fast, but emptied himself thereof."[1]

## STRIFE AND FACTION (Greek: eritheia/er-ith-i -ah)

**Strong's Concordance #2052:** intrigue, i.e. faction—contention, strife.

**Vine's Expository Dictionary:** contention, faction: denotes "ambition, self-seeking, rivalry," self-will being an underlying idea in the word; hence it denotes "party-making." It is derived, not from *eris,* "strife," but from *erithos,* "a hireling"; hence the meaning of "seeking to win followers," contention. It represents a motive of self-interest and is sometimes rendered selfishness.

**Webster's Dictionary:** A bitter sometimes violent conflict or dissension; an act of contention; fight, struggle, exertion, or contention for superiority.

**Use and Application:** Faction and strife have twin meanings denoting "ambition, self-seeking, rivalry," self-will being an underlying idea in the words; hence referring to factionalism, rivalry, and partisanship and pride that prompts people to push for their own way.

## VAINGLORY (Greek: kenodoxia\Ken-od-ox-ee-ah)

**Strong's Concordance #2754:** empty glorying, i.e. self-conceit: vain-glory.

**Vine's Expository Dictionary:** "Empty conceit" (*kenodoxia* from *kenos* = empty, vain, hollow, groundless; *doxa* = glory, praise, or opinion) is used only here in the New Testament and is translated in King James Version as "vainglory," which is defined as an excessive or ostentatious pride or "counting yourself better than others." The Revised Standard Version chose the word "conceit" to translate the Greek here. The New International Version translators rendered it "vain conceit."

**Webster's Dictionary:** excessive or ostentatious pride in one's achievements; vain display or show.

**Use and Application:** We speak of a vainglorious person as being conceited. "Nothing to gratify your own personal vanity" (Lightfoot); "and in search for empty glory" (Barclay). "Doing nothing impelled by empty pride" (Wuest). Note: faction and vainglory have been spoilers of the Church of God in all ages. Petty strivings for place and preferment, jockeying for advantage, pushing and shoving for prestige or attention—many congregations of believers in Christ have been blighted or destroyed by the sins Paul mentions.

# PRACTICAL APPLICATIONS

Let this mind be in you which is also in Christ Jesus (see Phil. 2:5). Since you have been transformed by the renewing of your mind, you now have the mind of Christ. With the mind of Christ Jesus, you do those things which He desires, as you think His thoughts, have His attitude, share His love, and exhibit His humility when He emptied Himself. Hence, you ask yourself, "What would Jesus do?" as you ponder specific applications and reflections to apply both the theological and philosophical lessons learned in order to:

- Adopt Christ's attitude of unselfishness, servanthood, humility, and obedience.

- Adopt attitudinal characteristics for maintaining unity and living unselfishly.

- Seek to be one in spirit with other members. The Church ought to be one in spirit because the Spirit of Christ unites the Church into one body.

- Understand the basis and importance of unity.

- Regard, consider, count, and esteem others as more important than self.

- Understand that giving up self for service to others is truly the power of a humble mind because humility with love brings honor and exaltation.

## ACTION STEPS

A. The first step is to prayerfully read and meditate on Philippians 2:1-11. As Christ Jesus willing laid aside His heavenly glory to come to earth and die, we should be willing to adopt Christ's attitude of unselfishness, servanthood, humility, and obedience and look beyond our own interest for the sake of others.

B. Think about what it means to have the mind-set of Christ. You must show evidence of selflessness and humility while considering the needs of others as your top priority.

1. Encourage and motivate others toward unity that produces joy.

2. Witness to others at home, work, while traveling, and in your daily living.

3. "Let nothing be done through selfish ambition or conceit." You are to avoid doing things with self-serving motives and discover ways to regard, consider, count, esteem, and show concern about the interests of others.

4. "In lowliness of mind you are to esteem others as being better than yourself." You are to esteem others as being more important and more worthy than you are and be willing to accept failings in others without looking down on them.

5. "Let each of you look out not only for his own interests, but also for the interests of others." You are to avoid self-centeredness and a spirit of selfishness as you look out for the interests of others instead of being completely absorbed in your own concerns and spiritual growth.

C. Conduct your life so that others may see you as a Gospel sermon— *Let this mind be in You which was also in Christ Jesus.*

1. Be humble, and in humility think more of others than you do of yourself. Never act from motives of rivalry or personal vanity.

2.  Cultivate a spirit of authentic Christian humility that would be evidenced by a willingness to regard others as more important than self.

3.  Show and express love toward other believers and non-believers—relatives, friends, neighbors, and coworkers. You are to humble yourself, and treat them with love and dignity because it is the right thing to do.

4.  Be humble, thinking of others as better than yourself. Don't be selfish; don't live to make a good impression on others.

5.  Give up self for service to others—truly the power of a humble mind.

D. Read First John 3:16 and reread Philippians 2:4-8 to understand that the sacrifice of Christ is both the proof of His love and the standard of our own love for others. Then ask yourself, "Am I willing to humble myself, even sacrifice myself, in the best interest of another?"

1.  Always ask yourself, "What would Jesus do?"

2.  Imagine Jesus doing the things that you are doing or thinking the things that you are thinking; then reflect on how you would compare Jesus' attitude and action to your attitude and action.

E. Read John 13:3-17 to understand that Jesus' act of washing the disciples' feet demonstrated love. Jesus was their teacher and Lord, meaning He was on a higher level than the disciples, yet He assumed a position of humility and service because He loved those He served.

1.  Practice being humble by serving others and committing yourself to doing things that you think are beneath you. Remember, you cannot have unity without humility, and you will not humble yourself for anybody you don't love.

2.  Perform a menial task to teach a lesson in humility and selfless service because, ultimately, servanthood is a disposition of the heart and spirit, which expresses itself in concrete action.

F.  Ask for wisdom to know the secret things of God. And His Spirit will reveal them to you, for you have the mind of Christ because the Spirit of Christ lives in you.

G.  Read and meditate on John 17:22. It is critical to understand that Christ Jesus also prayed for the future believers that they might be one.

H.  Recognize that it is what you put into practice from God's Word that brings blessings to you and others.

# PART FOUR

# FINDING PEACE THROUGH PRAISE

Our world is filled with anxiety, frustration, turmoil, and apprehension. There is concern for our families, finances, global terrorism, relationships, and a multitude of other matters, for which all seek peace. Yet peace often remains an elusive stranger that we long to befriend.

Contrary to what many people think, peace is not about mind-over-matter. You cannot talk your way into peace. Rather, it is when you take your eyes off yourself, your circumstances, and your world, and focus them on God that you will discover peace. In this section, you will discover that you can praise your way into peace.

When you begin to see yourself and your world through the eyes of God, you will tap into tranquility and true happiness. Once your thoughts have been transformed, so that you focus vertically rather than horizontally, peace like a river will flood your soul.

# CHAPTER SIXTEEN

# REJOICE ALWAYS

Think praise. In Philippians, God has commanded that we are to *"rejoice always"* (Phil. 4:4) and to think on things that give us peace, consolation, and victory, in spite of the circumstances we face in our lives. Accordingly, we find that the apostle Paul, though a prisoner, was exultantly happy and calls us to be full of joy and to rejoice always.

As we carefully read and review Philippians, we find that there is a connection between rejoicing and the power of the mind. In chapter 2 of Philippians, Paul tells us to *have* the mind of Christ (see Phil. 2:5), and as he is about to close, he says in chapter 4, *"Finally brethren...meditate on these things"* (Phil. 4:8). It appears that the power to think is the antibody, the antidote to anything that can happen in one's life.

There is no question that when Paul says, *"Rejoice in the Lord always. Again I will say, rejoice!"* (Phil. 4:4), he is not asking you to rejoice at certain times or in certain circumstances; he is commanding you to rejoice at *all* times. He detaches rejoicing from your circumstances as he sends out a carte blanche statement, an imperative command—*Rejoice, and again I will say, rejoice.* Without knowing what situations you will face and without conducting a survey, Paul sees you (with his spiritual eyes) hesitating and contemplating how to rejoice in negative situations. It is clear that he feels the need to repeat himself because of your hesitation. Essentially, he is saying, "Just in case you didn't hear me the first time, I will say it again—I want you to always give God an expression of jubilee. Rejoice, and again I will say, rejoice."

Paul says it again and again because we need to hear it again and again. We need to know that the joy of the Lord is so powerful; it can abound

151

even in the worst situations. It is imperative for you to understand that it does not matter what you have or what is happening in your life; you must know within your heart that you are special and that God indwells your mind through His Spirit.

Since you are connected to God through His Spirit, you can rejoice as you look through the eyes of faith to see that God has planned for you to praise, to worship, and to thank Him for His faithfulness, no matter how devastating the circumstances, because *"...the joy of the Lord is your strength"* (Neh. 8:10). The joy that comes from the Lord is what gives you ability and strength to overcome trials and to realize victories and to refuse to yield to what the flesh wants to do even when you're faced with discouraging circumstances. The Holy Spirit is telling you that your circumstances are not to dictate your attitude; rather, your praise claims that God is above the situation, and rejoicing becomes a lifelong occupation.

What does it mean to "rejoice always"? The word *rejoice* is an imperative, a command that comes from the word *joy*, a fruit of the Spirit. To rejoice is the central core of why you were created. God created us to give Him glory, and we are expected to always have joy as we give Him praise. Richard Baxter said, "May the Living God...make these, our carnal minds so spiritual, and our earthly hearts so heavenly, that loving Him, and delighting in Him, may be the work of our lives."[1]

Yes, Christians are commanded to rejoice under all circumstances, and obedience is possible because true joy is in the Lord. As believers, we can be inwardly joyful when everything around us is dreary. This means that you are to rejoice even when the doctor tells you that the diagnostic report reveals cancer in your body. Why? You rejoice and praise God for the healing process that is taking place in your body. You rejoice and praise God for overcoming the chemotherapy and radiation. You rejoice and praise God for the surgeon, anesthesiologist, nurse, orderly, medication, and everything that will be used for your treatment and complete healing. You rejoice and praise God because you have been transformed by the renewing of your mind, and you now have the mind of Christ. You look past the suffering to victory in healing, and you boldly declare:

*I know how to be abased, and I know how to abound. Everywhere and in all things I have learned both to be full and to be hungry, both to abound and to suffer need. I can do all things through Christ who strengthens me* (Philippians 4:12-13).

Paul's attitude teaches us an important lesson. Your inner attitude does not have to reflect your outward circumstances. Paul was full of joy because he knew that no matter what happened to him, Jesus Christ was with him. So when you encounter situations in which there seems to be no reason for happiness, you should always rejoice and delight in the Lord.

Similarly, in Second Corinthians 6:10, Paul encouraged us to be joyful: *"As sorrowful, yet always rejoicing; as poor, yet making many rich; as having nothing, and yet possessing all things."* Rejoicing is to be a constant discipline for those who are in Christ because we are aware that Jesus gives peace to those who trust Him and ask for His help. Moreover, true faith never says, "I cannot." You have the freedom to rejoice always. More importantly, you rejoice always because God has delivered you from the corruption and death in sin, and you have the promise that the Lord Jesus is coming soon.

Habakkuk also reminds us that when the circumstances of life present a negative picture of failure and loss, or when the natural reaction is grief or complaint, this is the time to put faith in God and in His Word.

*Though the fig tree may not blossom, nor fruit be on the vines; though the labor of the olive may fail, and the fields yield no food; though the flock may be cut off from the fold, and there be no herd in the stalls—yet I will rejoice in the Lord, I will joy in the God of my salvation* (Habakkuk 3:17-18).

Thus, when you ask—"How can I rejoice when life seems to be crushed by persecution, failures, negative experiences, or horrific circumstances?"— you can rejoice and praise God at the same time you are fighting the sinful nature of the flesh with the will of the spirit because the Spirit of Christ, the Living Water, is constantly flowing through your transformed and renewed mind. You can praise God that you have the victory over the devil because you have been released and you now have the mind of Christ.

# CHAPTER SEVENTEEN

## YOU ARE WHAT YOU THINK

Who are you? It is what you think about yourself that gives significance to who you are. What you think about yourself can elevate or decline your position. When you understand the equation of the thinking process, you will know that you are your thoughts, and your thoughts are somewhere within you. Thus, self-knowledge becomes significant to overall knowledge, and it is in the mind where you store what you think about yourself.

The question then is: Can someone be thinking of praising God, while at the same time, not thinking of joy and rejoicing? It does not seem possible, because when you deal with the concept of the mind, you cannot be separated from what you think, and you cannot think separately from yourself. Moreover, it is significant to understand that the mind is attached to the source, which is the power of God; while at the same time, the mind is also connected to the flesh—the body—and the body is connected to your environment, issues, and circumstances.

## WHAT IS THE MIND?

Remember that in the Old Testament, the word *mind* was translated from the Hebrew word *nephesh*, which means the total person—soul, spirit, and mind. Moreover, the words *mind* and *spirit* were often interchanged because the mind serves almost the same function as the spirit. In the New Testament, the Greek word used in this text for "mind" is *nous*, which is defined by *Strong's Concordance* as "the intellect, the mind in thought, feeling or will; the understanding." *Nous* is further defined as the total conceptual process of thinking.[1] In essence, your mind is more than your brain, your thought, your intellect, or your reason; it is the whole conceptual process that begins with the spirit that resides at the core of your being and ends with the life actions that are produced in the soul. In other words, your mind not only includes the conception or the creation of an idea, but your mind also causes you to act according to what is being produced in your spirit—your soul.

According to Descartes, dualism began as an awareness of listening to the soul, the still center and spiritual experience when he captured this profound self-awareness in the famous words, *Cogito, ergo sum*: "I think, therefore I am." Descartes then proceeded to develop his epiphany into a formal philosophy, which we now call Cartesian dualism. Modern philosophical theories of the mind are based on scientific understanding of the brain, and the *mind* is seen as a phenomenon of psychology. The term is often used more or less synonymously with consciousness.

More importantly, using your mind is rooted in biblical precept; in the New Testament, as a believer you are encouraged to:

- Love your God with all of your heart and with all of your soul and with all of your mind (see Matt. 22:37, Mark 12:30; Luke 10:27).

- Be of one mind (see Acts 4:32, 1 Cor. 1:10; 2 Cor. 13:11).

- Be transformed by the renewing of your minds, which is a process. In First Corinthians 14:15, Paul says that he will pray with his spirit and also with his mind; he will sing with his spirit and also with his mind.

- Come now, let us reason together, says the Lord (see Isa. 1:18).

Likewise, the Old Testament tells us, *"As he thinks in his heart, so is he"* (Prov. 23:7). The heart is symbolic of the mind, and your mind is who you are; your mind is the real you. It is, therefore, unrealistic to think that you are to rejoice only during pleasant circumstances and to worry or be anxious regarding issues and situations that are unpleasant or painful. It is also unrealistic to determine, "I am not supposed to think about a bad situation or an impending crisis"; for when danger presents itself, the mind must recognize it, whether it's spiritual or sensual (sinful in nature), and evaluate what must take place.

## YOUR MIND EVALUATES YOU

The mind is a place of evaluation, and in order to evaluate, you must be objective about subjective things. Your mind should rise above your thoughts as your spirit tells you what to do in all circumstances. Your mind must stay free in order to make judgments about who you are, what to do, where to go, and what to wear. Aristotle said, "In the soul which is called mind, that whereby the soul thinks and judges."[2] Your mind should be free from the contamination that makes it turn against you, because your mind is the only thing you have to protect you from your environment. You need to keep your mind free so that you are constantly aware of dangerous issues and circumstances that may come close to your body, mind, and spirit.

You should always reject negative thoughts from your mind because these thoughts will destroy you. When you think seriously about this, it is even better to allow poverty, sickness, or other uncontrollable circumstance to create problems in your life than for you to allow your mind to turn against you and eventually destroy you.

Good thoughts will ultimately lead to good thoughts about yourself, and bad thoughts will ultimately lead to bad thoughts about yourself. So when you are having problems with your circumstances, sooner or later it comes around to you. The more negatively you think, the more negative you become. And when you become negative, you reduce yourself rather than flourish, and ultimately, your thoughts become your greatest enemy. You cannot remain a positive person while thinking negatively.

It is, therefore, imperative that you understand that your mind is too powerful for you to allow it to turn against you. You can't afford to let your mind turn and work against you. You need your mind to fight the environmental battles, to stave off the evil spirits, to be a conduit for the power of God, to bring out your creativity, and to offset the negativity of your environment. You can't afford to think negativity in a negative situation. You are not to think yourself into sickness, poverty, non-productivity, and non-creativity. You have to think your way out of it.

The command is that we are to worship and rejoice in the Lord always. Notice Paul uses the perfect tense when he says, *"Be anxious* [careful] *for nothing..."* (Phil. 4:6). He is actually saying, "Don't continue to be anxious (careful) for anything." He is telling us to thank and praise God in the middle of our trials, because when we praise, we release our trials and tribulations to God.

## PRAISE RELEASES

Praise releases us, but negative condemnation, including negative thought and criticism, restricts and controls us. You must, therefore, be very careful to allow the spiritual mind to maintain control over negative thoughts that are being fed from the carnal mind or the mind of the flesh, which is connected to the world through your senses.

It is also good to know that as you are rejoicing and praising God, He is washing your mind of your trials and tribulations as He gives you the peace of God. When you release the negative thoughts, the Spirit of Christ guards you with His peace.

## CHAPTER EIGHTEEN

# DON'T WORRY, BE HAPPY

We have often heard the question, "Why worry when you can pray?" You may also remember the song, "Don't worry, be happy." We are not to worry because worrying is a device of the devil. When we worry, we are saying that we don't trust that God will provide for our needs. Most of us worry about things that will never happen or things that are of very little significance. We worry that we don't have the right kind of clothing. We worry about being with the right person; then we worry that we do not have a new car or enough money in the bank. Some of us even worry because we can't control other people.

Paul uses the perfect tense to tell us not to worry, but to worship instead. He says, *"Be anxious for nothing, but in everything by prayer and supplication, with thanksgiving, let your requests be made known to God"* (Phil. 4:6). The word *but* suggests a bold and strong contrast from *"Be anxious for nothing* [don't worry]*"* to the command to *pray.* The little word *but* cancels the first part of the statement—*"Be anxious for nothing"* or don't worry about anything.

Clearly, there is a definite connection between Philippians 4:6 and 4:8. Verse 6 says, *"Be anxious for nothing, but in everything by prayer and supplication, with thanksgiving, let your requests be made known to God."* And verse 8 says, *"Finally, brethren, whatever things are true...if there is any virtue and if there is anything praiseworthy—meditate on these things."* Verse 6 is a positive instruction against negativity, and verse 8 says you are to fix your thoughts—think on things that are true, honorable, right, pure, lovely, admirable excellent, and worthy of praise.

Prayer now replaces worry for the Christian believer; prayer is an anti-dote to worry. In essence, prayer combats worry by allowing us catharsis—spiritual renewal by purging our emotions, eliminating stress, releasing tension, and bringing us into expressions of praise, thanksgiving, and joy.

## FAITH AND PRAISE

Because worry and prayer cannot coexist, you must choose to be con-tented in all circumstances, pray in faith about what you need, and praise God for all He has done. There is clearly a relationship and spiritual con-nection between faith and praise—we are dealing with the substratum issues of the child of God, who is connected to God by faith; it is a spiri-tual connection. Two key points for you to remember are that faith is based on knowledge of God's Word and His character and that the spirit of the world is in opposition to God. Thus, when you stand in faith, the world loses its controlling influence over your mind.

The Hebrew word for "faith" (*emeth*) connotes faithfulness, which equals "trusted," "trustworthy," or "confidence and trust in God and in God's Word." It does not mean belief in a dogmatic sense. In the Greek, however, the word for "faith" is *pistis,* and primarily it conveys firm persua-sion, confidence, assurance, trustworthiness, or a conviction based upon hearing. Faith is, in general, the persuasion of the mind—that a state-ment or idea is true and worthy of trust. To understand this concept more clearly, we refer to the Bible passage, *"Now faith is the substance* [assurance, title-deed] *of things* [seen and unseen] *hoped for, the evidence* [proof, convic-tion] *of things not seen"* (Heb. 11:1).

The writer of Hebrews provides a description of how faith works instead of a definition of faith. The author stresses that faith is established convic-tion concerning things unseen and settled expectation of future reward. Faith is the title deed of things hoped for, and throughout Hebrews chapter 11, the author emphasizes that assurance rests on God's prom-ises. For example, *"that Christ may dwell in your hearts through faith...to know the love of Christ which passes knowledge..."* (Eph. 3:17-19). The love of Christ in its fullness is beyond all human comprehension, and not even the greatest minds of theology and philosophy can explain an understanding of God through reason and experimentation. It is only by faith that you come to know the love of Christ Jesus. Also, Romans 10:17 states, *"So then faith comes by hearing and hearing by the word of God."* Yet faith is not something that you produce; it is what God's Word produces in you.

The Bible is clear; Christ Jesus is our spiritual leader, and it is by faith that we follow Him. He tells us, *"Whoever desires to come after me, let him deny himself, and take up his cross, and follow Me"* (Mark 8:34). We are the sheep of His pasture, and we hear and know His voice as He speaks to us. We also know that Christ is the perfecter of our faith, and while on the cross, He said, *"It is finished!"* (John 19:30).

## PRAYER RELEASES WORRY

As Paul reminds us that we should not be anxious about anything, we can shout these words of victory. The Greek word for "anxious"—*merimna*—refers to concern that may become fretful and inappropriate if taken too far. Paul says that instead of being anxious and becoming distraught over a particular situation, we should take it to the Lord in prayer. Matthew 6:25-34 illustrates the worthlessness of worry by showing that it is unnecessary, unfruitful, and unbecoming to a Christian:

> *Therefore I say to you, do not worry about your life, what you will eat or what you will drink, not about your body, what you will put on... Look at the birds of the air, for they neither sow nor reap nor gather into barns; yet your heavenly Father feeds them. Are you not of more the value than they? Which of you by worrying can add one cubit to his stature? ...Therefore do not worry about tomorrow, for tomorrow will worry about its own thing. Sufficient for the day is its own trouble* (Matthew 6:25-27,34).

You can thank and praise God because you are connected to the Spirit of Christ, who you can pray to, instead of worry. Prayer now replaces worry.

Paul used several different Greek words for prayer in this verse. "Prayer" (*proseuche*) is the most general term for our communications to God. "Supplication" or "petition" (*deesis*) refers to requests for particular benefits. "Thanksgiving" (*eucharistia*) is grateful acknowledgment of past mercies. "Requests" (*aitemata*) looks at individual requests of God that form part of the whole prayer.

Supplication is more than petitioning; it also suggests an intensity of earnestness in extended prayer—not to gain merit by many words, but to fully transfer the burden of one's soul into God's hands. Prayer and peace are closely connected. One who entrusts cares to Christ instead of fretting over them will experience the peace of God to guard oneself from nagging anxiety.

Don't worry; pray. The word for "prayer" here is *proseuche*, and it means prayer as worship. Part of the antibody for worry is worship. With faith and prayer, we place our problems and worry into God's hands. Once your mind evaluates and determines a problem, you are to put the problem into God's hands. When you raise your hands in worship, you are to release anything that causes you to worry. Paul says, prayer is stressing a sense of need; prayer with a supplication request stresses thanksgiving for the object asked for. So when you worship and make your requests, you should immediately praise Him for the object of request. When you praise and worship Him, you release the cares of your mind to the One who is all-powerful. When you come to God, you free your mind from the negative. You ask Him for what you need and praise Him for giving it to you as you allow your mind to dwell on those things that will give you the victory.

## CHAPTER NINETEEN

# PRAISE BRINGS PEACE THAT TRANSCENDS UNDERSTANDING

Prayer and peace are closely connected. When you pray, you can push back the attack of your circumstances and your situation, defeat the tormenting thoughts in your mind, and claim the victory in order to experience peace of mind. If you pray rather than worry, God will give you peace, which transcends all powers of thought.

As for letting your requests be known to God, C.H. Spurgeon said:

> Cast your trouble where you have cast your sins; you have cast your sins into the depth of the sea, there cast your trouble also. Never keep a trouble half an hour on your own mind before you tell it to God. As soon as the trouble comes, quick, the first thing, tell it to your Father. Remember, that the longer you take telling your trouble to God. The more your peace will be impaired.[1]

In order to keep your mind focused on God, trusting in Him, you need to spend time in daily fellowship with Him. Isaiah declared unto God, *"Thou will keep him in perfect peace, whose mind is stayed on Thee; because he trusts in Thee"* (Isa. 26:3 KJV).

## THE PEACE OF GOD

The phrase "the peace *of* God" is peace that comes from God rather than peace *with* God. It is important to note that one may have peace with God without having the peace of God. Peace *with* God is dependent upon faith, whereas peace *of* God is a promise, which is the result of a thankful prayer to God. It is peace that comes to us—the tranquility of God's own presence—when we pray.

The peace of God actually describes your relationship with God. This peace is different from the world's peace. It is the peace that Jesus promised His disciples and all those who follow Him: *"Peace I leave with you; My peace I give to you; not as the world gives do I give to you. Let not your heart be troubled, neither let it be afraid"* (John 14:27). In Romans 5:1, Paul writes, *"Having been justified by faith, we have peace with God through our Lord Jesus Christ."* It is essential that you understand that true peace comes from knowing that God is in control and not just from positive thinking. As a believer, you have *"the peace of God, which surpasses all understanding, that will guard* [keep] *your hearts and minds through Christ Jesus"* (Phil. 4:7).

The Greek word for "guard," *phroureo*, is a military term that means to surround, protect, and keep a garrison or city. It is similar to soldiers standing guard, patrolling, or protecting a sentry or sanctuary against the enemy. You are in spiritual combat, guarded and protected by God's power and peace as your sentinels or patrols, surrounding the perimeter of your mind. Whenever or wherever there is a weak spot or area in your mind, God's peace is the soldier that guards that part of your mind so you can think positively in all circumstances. Thus, when the enemy attacks with a negative thought, the sentry guard moves to that position in your mind and begins to shut out every destructive thought from the devil. The peace of God counterattacks so you begin to think positively.

Remember, *"You are kept by the power of God through faith for salvation ready to be revealed in the last time"* (1 Pet. 1:5). You should always be aware that God's peace completely surrounds your heart, mind, emotion, appetite, soul, and spirit in order to secure you against satan's attacks and other harmful outside forces. And when you are thinking of the good things He has done, you will want to give Him thanks and praise.

## GIVING THANKS AND PRAISE

Even though you may think you have no reason to thank Him, the Bible says to do so. *"Giving thanks always for all things to God the Father in the name of our Lord Jesus Christ"* (Eph. 5:20). We give thanks because He is working everything together for our good (see Rom. 8:28).

It is His will that we give thanks: *"In everything give thanks: for this is the will of God in Christ Jesus for you"* (1 Thess. 5:18). You are to begin with thanksgiving.

> *Be careful for nothing; but in everything by prayer and suppli-cation with thanksgiving let your requests be made known unto God. And the peace of God, which passes all understanding, shall keep your hearts and minds through Christ Jesus* (Philippians 4:6-7 KJV).

In the Amplified Bible, Philippians 4:7 states,

> *And God's peace [shall be yours, that tranquil state of a soul assured of its salvation through Christ, and so fearing nothing from God, and being content with its earthly lot of whatever sort that is, that peace] which transcends all understanding shall garrison and mount guard over your hearts and minds in Christ Jesus* (AMP).

You can praise and thank God in all things and in all circumstances because *"God's peace shall be yours."* When you think of pure things, just things, lovely things, righteous things, honest things, and things of good report, you move to praise and thanksgiving.

As a Christian believer, you are connected to the Spirit of Christ, possessing the peace of God, which guards you from worries and anxieties. And with the peace of God, your mind is free to think praise. When you think praise, God keeps you in perfect peace because your mind is stayed on Him and because you trust in Him. Consequently, your future will be better than your past because peace in the heart will follow praying about your concerns.

Most of us have experienced lack of peace from time to time when we pray. Paul was not saying that you will feel absolutely at ease and relieved after you pray. Still, a measure of peace will be yours. You will have the confidence that you have laid the matter before the Lord and you trust

Him. Note that he does not promise peace as the indicator of God's will when you are praying about what you should do. Paul did not say that if you need to make a decision God will make His will known by giving you peace and joy about the right choice.

Once the joy arises, and joy is what you feel toward God, it brings you to a place of praise, and when you praise and rejoice in the midst of trials, you then release those trials and tribulations to God. As you do so, you release the negative thoughts and begin to think positively. When you rejoice and praise God, He guards your mind with His peace. So when you thank and praise God, your mind is washed and renewed in order for the peace of God to mount against your sinful desires.

Because God has connected your mind to His creative power, you must recognize from a personal point of view that every child of God has to become more spiritual in his or her thinking. It is significant then to understand that becoming spiritual in your thinking does not make you a religious fanatic; rather, it brings you into a closer relationship with the Spirit of God. Thus, you ought to keep your mind on the One who can do more for you than you can do for yourself. That's spiritual thinking.

It is critical to remember that because you have been transformed by the renewing of the mind, your thoughts are now connected to praise and glory. Praise is not dependent upon your feelings or emotions, it is: *"I will praise You, Lord, with all my heart..."* (Ps. 9:1 NIV). *"I will extol the Lord at all times; His praise will always be on my lips"* (Ps. 34:1 NIV). You are to always rejoice and think praise.

Paul reminds you that through praising and rejoicing you have been transformed by the renewing of the mind, and with your renewed mind you are identifying God as being above your situations as you worship God in Spirit and truth. It is through your worship that you are able to identify God for who He is and what He does. You are transformed by the renewing of your mind.

## REASONS TO REJOICE

You are now "out of the box," and you can boldly proclaim, "I am now liberated and free; no longer trapped in the box of negative and destructive thinking." You are to give God praise because He loves us so much that He gave His only begotten Son, and because of His blood, you have been washed into righteousness.

When you are connected to the Spirit of Christ, you can personally say:

- I have the desire and the will to be creative, victorious, and the best I can be.
- I must not allow my thoughts to overpower my will.
- I will not allow others to control my will by controlling my mind or my thoughts.
- I can do all things because the Spirit of Christ has renewed my mind.
- I can now change my circumstances.
- I am a child of God. The Lord Jesus is my Savior, and I belong to Him.
- I am in Christ and not under condemnation.
- I am healed, delivered, and set free.
- I am transformed, and I have a renewed mind.

You rejoice because you have the mind of Christ, and with the mind of Christ, you can say, "The Spirit of the Lord God is upon me, because the Lord has anointed me; He has sent me to bring glad tidings to the lowly, to heal the brokenhearted, to proclaim liberty to the captives and release to the prisoners, to announce a year of favor from the Lord" (see Isa. 61:1-2).

Giving up self for service to others is truly the power of a humble mind because humility with love brings honor and exaltation. The humiliation and exaltation of Christ are lessons for all believers:

> As Christ ceased not to be a King because He was a servant, nor to be a lion because he was like a lamb, nor to be God because He was made a man, nor to be a judge because He was judged; so a man does not lose his honor by humility, but he shall be honored for his humility.[2]

Does your life demonstrate a Christ-like humility that God will delight to honor by exaltation? If so, then you can boldly proclaim:

- I am beautiful, extraordinary, magnanimous, and very special to God.

- I am blessed and anointed.

- I am rejoicing and praising God at all times.

- I have the mind of Christ, and the Spirit of Christ dwells in me.

- I think like Christ; I am a winner.

- I can win all mind games through Christ who strengthens me.

- Rejoice, and again I say, rejoice.

We are to:

*Rejoice* because Christ Jesus loved us and He laid down His life for us.

*Rejoice* because we are redeemed from sin with the precious blood and sacrificial death of Christ.

*Rejoice* because God gives us His love that surpasses all understanding.

*Rejoice* because Jesus said, *"...If you loved Me, you would rejoice because I said, 'I am going to the Father,' for My Father is greater than I"* (John 14:28).

*Rejoice* and be exceedingly glad, for great is our reward in Heaven.

Rejoice in the Lord!

# CHAPTER TWENTY

# THEOLOGICAL AND PHILOSOPHICAL THOUGHTS AND CONCEPTS

## REJOICE AND BE CONTENTED IN ALL CIRCUMSTANCES.

*Never lose the power to think on things that give you peace, consolation and victory in spite of the circumstances you face in your life.*

| THEOLOGY | PHILOSOPHY |
| --- | --- |
| Be full of joy...rejoice! It seems strange that a man in prison would be telling a church, people who are free, to keep on rejoicing. He stresses to them the joy that they ought to have because of their relationship with God. Paul was full of joy because he knew that no matter what was happening in his life, he would be free if he kept his mind on Christ Jesus. Scripture is clear—we are to never lose the power to think on things that give us peace, consolation, and victory in spite of the circumstances we face in life. Philippians 4:4—*"Rejoice in the Lord always. Again I will say rejoice!"* | Saint Aquinas—"Man cannot live without joy; therefore when he is derived of true spiritual joys it is necessary that he become addicted to carnal pleasures."[1] Aristotle—"Suffering becomes beautiful when anyone bears calamities with cheerfulness, not through insensibility but...." "The ideal man bears the accidents of life with dignity and grace, making the best of circumstances."[2] Kant—"It is not God's will merely that we should be happy, but that we should make ourselves happy."[3] |

## REJOICE AND BE CONTENTED IN ALL CIRCUMSTANCES.

*Never lose the power to think on things that give you peace, consolation and victory in spite of the circumstances you face in your life.*

| THEOLOGY | PHILOSOPHY |
|---|---|
| Luke 10:20—*"Rejoice because your names are written in heaven."* | Spurgeon—"Trials teach us what we are; they dig up the soil, and let us see what we are made of."[4] |
| Romans 12:12—*"Rejoicing in hope, patient in tribulation, continuing steadfastly in prayer."* | "Thee Lord gets his best soldiers out of the highlands of affliction."[5] |
| Romans 15:13—*"Now may the God of hope fill you with all joy and peace in believing that you may abound in hope by the power of the Holy Spirit."* | Calvin—"There is not one blade of grass, there is no color in this world that is not intended to make us rejoice."[6] |
| Galatians 5:22—*"But the fruit of the Spirit is love, joy, peace."* | Marcus Aurelius: "When you arise in the morning, think of what a precious privilege it is to be alive—to breathe, think, to enjoy, to love."[7] |
| Philippians 2:17-18—*"If I am being poured out as a drink offering on the sacrifice and service of your faith, I am glad and rejoice with you all. For the same reason you also be glad and rejoice with me."* | Pascal—"The strength of a man's virtue should not be measured by his special exertions, but by his habitual acts."[8] |
| | Calvin—"You must submit to supreme suffering in order to discover the completion of joy.[9] |
| Colossians 1:11-12—*"Strengthened with all might, according to His glorious power, for all patience and longsuffering with joy; giving thanks to the Father."* | Martin Luther—"No man ought to lay a cross upon himself, or to adopt tribulation...but if a cross or tribulation come upon him, then let him suffer it patiently, and know that it is good and profitable for him."[10] |
| Colossians 1:24—*"I now rejoice in my sufferings for you* [your sake]." | C.S. Lewis—"Some people feel guilty about their anxieties and regard them as a defect of faith but they are afflictions, not sins. Like all afflictions, they are, if we can so take them, our share in the passion of Christ."[11] |

# MEANINGS AND EXPLANATIONS WITH USE AND APPLICATION

## ANXIOUS = CARE (Greek: merimna\mer-im-nsh)

**Strong's Concordance #3308:** to divide, "the mind." The word denotes distractions, anxieties, burdens, and worries.

**Vine's Expository Dictionary:** Signifies to be anxious about, to have a distracting care.

**Webster's Dictionary:** characterized by extreme uneasiness of mind or brooding fear about some contingency: Worried, resulting from or causing anxiety.

**Use and Application:** means to be anxious beforehand about daily life. Such worry is unnecessary because the Father's love provides for both our daily needs and our special needs.

## PRAISE (Greek: epainos\ep-ahee-nos)

**Strong's Concordance #1868:** superimposition, as a relation of distribution. Laudation, a commendable thing: praise.

**Vine's Expository Dictionary:** Denotes "approbation, commendation, praise"; it is used of those on account of, and by reason of, whom as God's heritage, "praise" is to be ascribed to God, in respect of His glory (the exhibition of His character and operations), of whatever is praiseworthy.

**Webster's Dictionary:** An expression of approval; commendation; worship; to glorify (a god or saint) by the attribution of perfections.

**Use and Application:** *Epainos* expresses not only praise for what God does for us, but also for who He is, recognizing His glory.

## PRAYER (Greek: proseuche\pros-yoo-khay)

**Strong's Concordance #4335:** prayer (worship); by implication, an oratory prayer.

**Vine's Expository Dictionary:** Denotes prayer to God, "to ask" should make a request. Also, (Greek: *deesis*) primarily "a wanting, a need, "an asking, entreaty, supplication."

**Webster's Dictionary:** An address (as petition) to God or a god in word or thought.

**Use and Application:** It is important to note that the word *prayer* has several meanings and uses. Starting with the noun, (Greek: *euche, proseuche, deesis, eneuxis*), which are prayers to God that also includes making a vow, the word expands to the verb (Greek: *euchomal*), a special term describing an invocation, request, or entreaty. Adding *pros,* "in the direction of God, (Greek: *proseuchomal*), makes the most frequent word for prayer.

## REJOICE (Greek: chairo\khak´-ee-ro)

**Strong's Concordance #5463:** To be cheerful, i.e. calmly happy or well-off; salutation (on meeting or parting), be well; farewell, be glad, God speed, greeting, hail joy, rejoice.

**Vine's Expository Dictionary:** "To rejoice; rejoicing in the Lord and in His presence; the rejoicing of others.

**Webster's Dictionary:** To give joy; to gladden; to feel joy or great delight.

**Use and Application:** *Chairo* describes a joy that is rejoicing, and to rejoice is to be glad or be gratefully happy.

# PRACTICAL APPLICATIONS

## "REJOICE IN THE LORD ALWAYS"

We are commanded to rejoice under all circumstances, and obedience is possible because true joy is in the Lord, and we must refuse to worry about things because Christ Jesus gives peace to those who trust Him and ask for His help.

We are to put into practice lessons learned from theology and philosophy in order to:

- Rejoice and be contented in all circumstances. This joy is to be experienced *always*.

- Understand that rejoicing is a constant discipline.

- Understand that we rejoice because true joy is in the Lord.

## ACTION STEPS

A. Prayerfully and carefully read the Book of Philippians (only four short chapters). This book is truly a masterpiece full of tenderness, warmth, affection, joy, and rejoicing.

B. Memorize Philippians 4:4-7 and allow the truth of the text to order your thinking and your life. The ultimate purpose is for you to love God with your mind and to trust Him at all times.

C. Rejoice in spite of trials.

1. Pray and thank the Lord for taking you through this situation.

2.  Praise God for who He is and what He has already done for you.

3.  *"Praise the Lord for the Lord is good; sing praises to His name, for it is pleasant"* (Ps. 135:3).

4.  *"Sing aloud to God our strength; make a joyful shout to the God of Jacob"* (Ps. 81:1).

D. If you have done something you should not have done, or if you have not done what you should have done, then you are to:

- Confess your sin because, *"If we confess our sins, He is faithful and just to forgive us our sins and to cleanse us from all unrighteousness"* (1 John 1:9).

- Pray as though everything depends on God; at the same time, you are to do all that you can to change the situation.

E. Rejoice in the joy of others. Rejoice when others are blessed and honored.

1.  Let your gentleness be known to all people. The Lord is at hand. Everyone who comes into contact with you should experience gentleness, moderation, and patience.

2.  Show respect for family members and close friends, not just the people you're trying to influence spiritually.

3.  Be gentle and kind to everyone and practice saying nice things to friends, family, and strangers.

4.  Give a word of encouragement and show appreciation for the little things.

5.  Be responsible and let other people know that they can depend upon you.

F. Reasons to rejoice and offer praise:

1.  Rejoice because God commands you to rejoice always.

2.  Rejoice because Christ Jesus loves you and He died for your salvation.

3.  Praise God verbally for who He is and what He has done.

4.  Remember, God's written Word is always relevant, powerful, and alive. The Word says, *"Rejoice in the Lord always. Again I will say rejoice"* (Phil. 4:4). Don't forget the word *always*.

5.  Believe that God loves you and He will never leave you. Knowing that God loves you and that He wants to communicate with your spirit gives you the strength to carry on—no matter what difficulties you are facing. Just knowing that *"...the joy of the Lord is your strength"* (Neh. 8:10) will bring peace and comfort at all times and in all circumstances.

6.  When you encounter a situation that is stressful or difficult and you don't feel happy, you can still be joyful on the inside as you rejoice and delight in the Lord.

# BATTLE FOR THE MIND

# PREFACE

We suggest that this study guide be used after reading *Battle for the Mind* in its entirety. Once you have gained the full scope of the content and principles, it will be of benefit to reread the text and use the questions and application materials to thoroughly digest its principles and put them to Kingdom use. The study guide can be used individually or in a group setting. Some of the applications involve research. A standard dictionary, a concordance, and a Bible dictionary are all tools that can be found on various Christian Websites. Some of the applications set goals that will include follow-up well after you have finished this study guide. In order to remind yourself to check up on your progress, we suggest you use your weekly planner, calendar, or journal to put reminders before you.

SECTION ONE

# BECOMING A SPIRITUAL PERSON

Read Section One in *Battle for the Mind*.

## THING TO PONDER

After opening with a brief discussion regarding the postmodern world, the authors concluded with the statement: "In the postmodern world there is no anchor, no foundation."

- What does this statement mean to you?
- Do you find this to be true in your experience?
- Has there been an anchor or foundation in other eras of history?
- What has created this void in our world?

## THING TO RESEARCH

1. Define the word *soul*. Use a standard American dictionary and a Bible dictionary to bring fullness to your understanding.

2. Ask a few people you know (Christians and non-Christians) what they think of the statement, "The world is looking for its soul."

| COMPARE THEIR IDEAS WITH YOUR OWN THOUGHTS *"The world is looking for its soul"* | |
|---|---|
| THOUGHTS AND IDEAS FROM OTHERS | MY THOUGHTS |
|  |  |

What did you learn from their comments?

## THINGS TO DO

Identify and define your unique qualities as you see them. Try not to let others' opinions or judgments about you enter into your thoughts. Include "natural" talents and abilities, character traits and personality distinctions, your experiences, your inherent tendencies, your passions, your spiritual gifts, and any other individual qualities you see. My unique qualities are (make a list):

## THINGS TO PRAY

The authors tell us that "if we can conquer the mind, we can find our uniqueness and begin to express our original self without the restraint of preconceived opinions and judgments." Spend time asking the Lord to release you from anything that would block you from understanding your original self. Ask the Holy Spirit to begin paving the way toward true spirituality.

## THINGS TO REACH FOR (Goals)

Goal: Read *Battle for the Mind* and work through the entire Study Guide.

- Sketch out a reasonable amount of time over the next weeks for reading and studying *Battle for the Mind*. Think through your time commitments and priorities.

- Set a goal as to how much of the material you would like to study in one week. When is the best time of the day to study? Which day of the week is best?

- Block out the times you have picked on your weekly planner so that you are reminded of your goals. Build in extra time for unforeseen events and detours that the Lord may plan for you to take.

INTRODUCTION

# THE STREET THAT LEADS TO SUCCESS—TRUTH FROM THE BOOK OF ROMANS

Read the Introduction to Section One in *Battle for the Mind*.

## THINGS TO PONDER

1.  "The mind is the seat of all spiritual and carnal conflict."

    - What do you think the authors mean by this statement?

    - Are you constantly battling sin within your thought life? How do your emotions and will fit into this conflict?

    - Have you become numb to sin through overexposure to the point that your mind ignores its presence? Are you hyper-aware of sin? Or are you somewhere in between?

2.  What have you learned through conflicts in your past experiences? Think through the details of what happened and explain how you believe God replaced the old mind with a new mind so that you desire spiritual things. (Reread "The Altar Within You.")

3.  Compare and contrast the mind of the spirit with the mind of the flesh; then answer the questions below:

| MIND OF THE SPIRIT | MIND OF THE FLESH |
|---|---|
|  |  |

- How can you tell the difference between the mind of the spirit and the mind of the flesh?

- Have you had Jesus shine a Light on your mind? If so, explain your experience.

- How do your weaknesses and human faults leave room for God's power?

4.   Paul cautions religious Jews that over self-confidence can be dangerous in Roman 2:19.

- What signs did the Jews have that they were becoming too self-confident?

- Have you ever relied more on yourself than on God? Explain or give specific examples.

5.   Do you think things will continually get better the more mature you become in God? Why or why not?

6.   Do you agree with the authors that "there is always going to be a struggle, even with the matchless grace of God and with this enormous power working on our behalf." Why or why not?

- If so, is God's grace outmatched by your struggles?

- How do you explain your continued propensity to be challenged throughout your life?

## THINGS TO RESEARCH

1.   Ask at least ten people to tell you what has been their greatest conflict since becoming a Christian; then continue the discussion with the following:

- Did they have the misconception that Christianity would produce a life of bliss.

- How does the Gospel need to be presented so that it is not a "bait-and-switch" promise of the good life, which delivers conflict instead?

2.   Compare the Book of Romans to the Four Gospels. The authors give you a starting point with the unique facets of the books. Take this a step further. Skim through the chapter headings of at least one of the Gospels and the Book of Romans; then add any other findings or concepts of:

- Your deeper understanding of Christ in the Gospel of _____ Your deeper understanding of Christ in the Book of Romans.

3.   "Thus, evil is not contradictory to grace as it is to the law." What does this mean? First, look up the word *evil* in a standard dictionary and in a Bible dictionary. Then do the same for *law* and for *grace*.

Explain the authors' statement based on your findings.

## THINGS TO DO

1.   Memorize Romans 8:6: *"For to be carnally minded is death, but to be spiritually minded is life and peace."* Write this Scripture out. Place it where you can be reminded of the rewards that will come as you renew your mind.

2.   Think about this statement in terms of your own experience. "The process of moving from the external (depending on a lot of outside sources) to the internal (depending on God and you) can be chaotic at best."

- Where are you in this process?

- Create an accountability day once a month that can help you determine your progress toward becoming more internally dependent.

- Circle the first day of each month on your calendar for the rest of the year in a particular color that will remind you to come before God and determine your progress.

## THINGS TO PRAY

1.   Take an extended amount of time to have a "Prayer Wrestling Match." Reread Romans 7:17-25. Take a piece of paper and create two

columns. The first column, label "The Good." Label the second column "The Evil." Write the phrases from the passage that fit into the specific column that applies. Now, at the bottom of the first column, write "The Mind," and at the bottom of the second column write "The Flesh."

| THE GOOD | THE EVIL |
|---|---|
| (List phrases of the Spirit) | (List phrases of the flesh) |
| The Mind | The Flesh |

Note: If you are going to really mean business in transforming your mind, you must be tenacious in your desire to change. Give a one-two punch to the flesh and the evil that it serves by committing yourself in prayer to walk in the *good*. Allow the Lord to give you a vision of what your mind can be like once you learn how to release yourself to His mind-set.

2. "The only altar on which you can lay your troubles is the altar within you." Have you surrendered all the present conflicts you face? Take time to identify and list burden/s that you would like to release to God; then meet with God at the altar within you so that you can release your burdens to Him and be refreshed.

## THINGS TO REACH FOR (Goals)

Goal: Use this book and study guide to renew your mind and to win the battle over it. You have been given the authors view of the "Romans Road." Now it's your turn. Read the Book of Romans this week. Use some sticky notes to jot down specific examples from your own life that relate to the passages as you read them, and tag them next to the appropriate verses. Some of these may be victories; some may be current challenges; some may be past defeats.

Your goal: By the end of this study, you will be able to look back on these sticky notes and re-evaluate how you are winning more battles with your renewed mind.

PART ONE

# OUT OF THE BOX

Read the Introduction to Part One of *Battle for the Mind*.

## THINGS TO PONDER

What are the things that keep you from becoming a spiritual person? Draw a large box at the bottom of this paper. Label the sides of your box by the specific inputs in your life that box you in—i.e. religion, negative words spoken into your life, harmful experiences, failure, interactions with people, and so forth. Why do you think you have assigned these things the power to control your spirituality?

CHAPTER ONE

# SURVIVING THE MINE FIELDS

Read Chapter One in *Battle for the Mind*.

## THINGS TO PONDER

1.   "It is critical for you to recognize that the flesh and the Spirit are in constant conflict because the mind of sinful flesh sets its desires against the mind of the Spirit. Thus, the mind becomes the battleground." Fill in the center column of the chart below; from your experience with these battles, classify the characteristics of the warfare you encountered.

| SPIRIT | WARFARE WAGED | FLESH |
|---|---|---|
| Grace | | Law |
| God | | satan |
| Revelation | | Situation |
| Spirit | | Flesh |
| Word | | World |

2.   In your own words, write an explanation of the meaning of Romans 8:1. Be sure to include who this verse addresses.

## THINGS TO RESEARCH

1.   "Whoever or whatever controls your mind controls you." Make a list of those things that seem to control you. Now, ask someone who knows you well and will be honest with you to list what they see that controls your mind. Compare your lists. How many of the items match? Be humble and open to the Holy Spirit as you search out your weaknesses.

The authors tell us that your mind is your life, your soul, your appetite, your person, and *you*—the total person. Also, "The 'mind' is...most commonly used to describe the higher functions of the human brain....such as personality, thought, reason, memory, intelligence, and emotion."

Look up the word *mind* in a standard dictionary and a Bible dictionary. Look up verses that deal with the mind in a concordance and answer the following questions:

- Do you think most people understand the composite nature of the mind? Explain.

- Explain why the mind is much more than your intellect and knowledge?

## THINGS TO DO

1.   Declare this week to be "Eliminate Katakrima Week." "The Greek word for 'condemnation'—*katakrima*—means to speak against your experiences. Condemnation (*katakrima*) makes you, the believer, feel negative about self in the midst of what God is doing for you in the struggle." At the top of each day in your planner, or on a sticky note placed on your computer, write *katakrima* and put a slash through it. Use this as a reminder to put every negative circumstance, whether you created it or not, in the positive light of God's plan for you.

2.   Memorize Colossians 3:2: *"Set your mind on things above, not on things on the earth."* Use this verse to remind yourself that if you set your mind on things above, you can resist operating in the realm of your "natural environment and not be controlled by the limitations of sinful flesh."

## THINGS TO PRAY

1.   "Self-condemnatory thinking actually causes you to aid and abet the negative satanic forces that are working through your sensual perceptions in order to defeat your faith. Remember, guilt and faith are opposing forces."

- How are you aiding and abetting the enemy?

- Are there patterns or situations that tend to illicit guilt from you? If so, confess these tendencies and ask for forgiveness. As you repent, ask the Holy Spirit to "build you up in the faith" so that you will repel guilt in the future.

2.   The authors remind us "...the soul of a man is connected to the very breath of God; and as soon as you become a living soul, your spirit and mind are connected to God."

- Begin to thank God for breathing into you so that you became a living soul.

- Spend some time "breathing in" the Holy Spirit and connecting your mind to God.

## THINGS TO REACH FOR (Goals)

Goal: Six months from now, you will have spiritually grown in a measurable way. "Maturity is now defined as the continued process of walking according to the Spirit while overcoming the flesh." Remember that the "battle being fought in the mind has nothing to do with your level of maturity...the key is your position in Christ."

- Define *maturity* in your own words.

- What is one mark of maturity that you hope others will notice in you six months from now?

- How will you remind yourself to pray for and seek this area of growth?

- How will you know if you have accomplished your goal?

CHAPTER TWO

# CONNECTING TO GOD AND TO THE WORLD AROUND YOU

Read Chapter Two in *Battle for the Mind*.

## THINGS TO PONDER

1. "God's Word describes two kinds of minds—the carnal...and the spiritual."

- What are some descriptive words that you could choose to describe the carnal mind?

- How might you describe the spiritual mind?

Many people think that spiritual warfare is waged solely in the heavenly realms. How do the authors show that spiritual warfare is waged in the mind?

- Why is it waged there?

- How does satan use your senses to get to your mind?

2. "In addition to pleasant and unpleasant circumstances leaving imprints on your mind, satan will also insert thoughts of sexual impurity, lust, and mental sexual fantasies in your mind."

- Have you ever wished that "God would just disconnect your flesh"?

- Why doesn't God just shut down the desires of the flesh?

- What purpose do they serve?

3. What is *revelation*? (See Chapter Two, and then define *revelation* in your own words).

- How did God give revelation to John the apostle? To Daniel? To Balaam? To Jesus?

- How does God give revelation to you?

- How does God's Spirit communicate to your spirit—to your mind through the Word?

- How does revelation keep your mind from being bound by past experiences and situations?

- How is it possible to not rely on situations, but to live by revelation?

4.   In Genesis Chapter 3, satan targeted Eve's senses of hearing, sight, touch, taste, and smell.

- Which of the five senses seems to get you into the most trouble?

- How are you limited because of your senses?

- Why don't your senses limit the way God can speak and commune with you?

- "While we are connected to the world through the senses, we do not come to God through our senses." How do we come to God? Why?

5.   Romans 10:17—*"So then faith comes by hearing* [the message], *and hearing by the Word of God."* Moreover, "we can depend upon God's Word to penetrate through horrific circumstances, bad situations, and failures of the past."

- How important is it to read, memorize, and meditate on the Word?

- How well do you do in these areas?

## THINGS TO RESEARCH

1.   The authors quote Descartes when discussing how the mind is deceived. What is *deception*? Look this word up in a standard dictionary. Then take a concordance and look up *deceive, deceived, deception,* and some of their corresponding key verses.

- Describe the process of deception in your own words.

- How does deception start, and where does it come from?

- Who is most susceptible to deception?

- What are some results of a deceived mind, and what do you think can break deception's hold on the mind?

2.   "It is in the mind where the imprints of positive and negative experiences are embedded. And when you don't erase the negative experiences from the mind, it can lead to mental and emotional disorders."

- How seriously should you take the authors' admonition to erase the indelible negative imprints on your mind so that your future will not be crippled?

3.   Use the Internet to research a few of the top newspapers stories about normal-looking people who have committed heinous crimes. Neighbors, friends, and family often are shocked because they thought the person was good on the outside and seemed normal. Explain in your own words, "How does a person go from 'normalcy' to becoming mentally unstable?"

## THINGS TO DO

1.   Memorize this Scripture: *"Because the carnal mind is enmity against God; for it is not subject to the law of God, nor indeed can be"* (Rom. 8:7). Think back on the times when you were thinking carnally about situations and relationships and explain how that puts you at enmity with God.

2.   Look up Scriptures that list the desires of the flesh. List them below and determine how you can overcome, manage, and maintain control over the desires of your flesh?

| DESIRES OF THE FLESH (list and circle the three that plague you the most). | HOW CAN YOU OVERCOME, MANAGE, AND MAINTAIN CONTROL OVER YOUR DESIRES |
|---|---|
|  |  |

## THINGS TO PRAY

Negative thoughts can make you experience feelings of condemnation, guilt, shame, depression, and/or unworthiness. You can also have scars from low self-esteem, dishonesty, and lack of trust that are internal tormenting thoughts that people do not see on the outside. If you have experienced any of these, you are to:

- Find a person whom you can trust to listen to the circumstances surrounding these hurts. Ask the person ahead of time to be prayerful and to not be sympathetic with you, but to help steer you to the Word of God and its healing.

- Take time to confess that you have accepted these negative thoughts and ask the Lord to remove these and help you to forget them. Then bask in God's love to replace these negative attitudes with the positive life of Kingdom living.

## THINGS TO REACH FOR (Goals)

1.   Goal: Do not let a negative idea attach itself and become embedded in your mind. How can you achieve this goal? First look at the process satan uses:

- An adverse situation or circumstance arises.

- You have a negative thought.

- You muse on the negative thought.

- The negative thought attaches itself.

- Your mind becomes embedded with that thought.

- Low self-esteem or depression increase and attach to the adverse situation or circumstance in your life.

- Additional tormenting thoughts arise.

- The cycle continues to escalate.

Next, find a Scripture for each part of this process that can jolt your mind out of the words of the world and into the Word of God. The next time a personal crisis occurs, pull out this page and find where you are in the process and feast on the Scripture you wrote beside that step. Stop the process dead in its tracks!

2.   Goal: Submit one current crisis or stressful situation to the Rhema Word from God's Spirit to your spirit. "The Spirit of Christ is seeking to control your mind...God doesn't always change your situation; He changes your mind." Use this as a byword for the situation you choose to submit to God's Spirit.

  - Journal your process of submission by writing notes about any significant event or revelation as you ask God to change your mind and not the situation. Remember, "God wants you, the believer, to know that if He changes your mind, then you can change your situation."

CHAPTER THREE

# THINKING AFFECTS YOUR TALKING AND WALKING

Read Chapter Three in *Battle for the Mind*.

## THINGS TO PONDER

1.  What is the difference between the "inner mind" and the "outer part of the mind"?

- Explain how the outer mind and the mouth are related?

- How does the mouth express a person's character and disposition?

- How do the inner mind and the outer mind relate to each other (use an example, such as the way the authors illustrated our praise to God)?

2.  The authors tell us that when God blows His Spirit into you, He is releasing you from your flesh, because your flesh will kill your vision.

- What does this mean to you?

- How can you stay connected to God so that you can reach into the Spirit and speak the Word to break the power of the enemy all around you?

3.  What is the "law of the Spirit"?

- Explain the regulative principle of the Holy Spirit.

- How does the Spirit exercise control over the life of the believer?

- Have you experienced the energy that comes from the Spirit, which takes you to the next level and enables you to do the will of the Father?

## THINGS TO RESEARCH

1.    Research the word *heart* in terms of the internal nature of a person and not the physical organ. Look up the word in a standard dictionary and a Bible dictionary.

- How is the word *heart* interchangeable with the word *mind*?

- How does the phrase *the voice of the heart* relate?

2.    Look up the Hebrew word *ruah* in a concordance and choose several Scriptures to read that use this word. Then look up the Greek word *pneuma* in the concordance and select some verses to read that contain this word.

- From these verses, describe the relationship between spirit and breath.

- Why do you need to understand the trinity in order to understand how your spirit and breath relate?

## THINGS TO DO

1.    Share the following thoughts with someone significant in your life. Ask this person to feed back to you what you have said in that person's own words so that you can see if you truly have understood these statements.

- "When God sets His mind on something, He sets His mind on it through your mind."

- "When God's Spirit blows His thoughts into your mind, then the will of God must come to pass."

- "When the Spirit of Christ moves in your life, you will no longer be manipulated through your flesh."

2.    Memorize Proverbs 23:7—*"As he thinks in his heart, so is he...."* Let this verse be a watchman to you in order for you to become disciplined in entertaining only thoughts that are noble and worthy of praise.

## THINGS TO PRAY

1.    Take the time to wait before the Lord to hear His still small voice.

- Pray that the Lord will find you a receptacle for His thoughts.

2.   Allow time for the Holy Spirit to blow into your spirit. Tell the world and satan the following statements:

- I am coming out; I can't stay in the box.

- I have to come out; I am tired of being restricted, held back.

- I am coming out of poverty, depression, and low self-esteem.

- I will never be the same because I am moving in the power of my anointing.

- I am liberated.

- I am free.

- No weapon formed against me shall prosper.

- I am empowered to defeat satan and walk according to the Spirit.

- I am no longer restricted by the carnal mind.

- I am no longer under the law, but under grace.

- I do not owe the flesh any favors; I am a debtor to the Holy Spirit.

## THINGS TO REACH FOR (Goals)

Goal: Hear the thoughts of God and give expression to them. Think about what the authors say when they tell us, "God talks much because He thinks much. And because God has so much to tell us, He blows His thoughts into our bodies to make us living thoughts."

How can you improve on hearing God's voice? Write the word *Listen* in black letters on a paper and attach it to the dashboard in your car. Place a small notepad and a pen in the passenger seat. When you are driving alone, instead of turning on the radio, make your drive a time to listen to God's voice. After you have arrived at your destination, jot down anything your spirit heard from God's Spirit, and make a plan to express those thoughts in some way during the next few hours. For example, if you heard God tell you to be more loving, you should express it through as many loving acts as possible in the next two hours. Or, if God spoke revelation to a crisis or situation, act on it by praying or by repairing what is needed.

CHAPTER FOUR

# FREEING YOURSELF FROM THE BOX

Read Chapter four in *Battle for the Mind*.

## THINGS TO PONDER

1.  "The flesh is never good enough. It is too restricting; your thoughts and your will have now been elevated beyond your situations."

- When you have tasted the spiritual way of accomplishing goals, why is it hard to be satisfied in the flesh?

- Have you felt that you accomplished something significant and yet, despite the achievement, felt unfulfilled?

2.  Read Romans 8:11—"*But if the Spirit of Him who raised Jesus from the dead dwells in you, He who raised Christ from the dead will also give life to your mortal bodies through His Spirit who dwells in you.*"

- Rewrite this Scripture using the personal pronoun *me*.

- How does this logical deduction work?

- Do you truly believe it? If not, what can help you to build your faith and believe God at His Word?

3.  "When you are in Christ and have been released into the power of God, then you can walk in His Spirit because you are:

- Free to rise up above your circumstances. (What circumstances are you facing today? How can you rise above them?)

- Free to be a powerhouse in the middle of a dying world. (What is your realm of influence where you make a difference in other people's lives? How can you walk with more power?)

- Free to speak things as they are and bring them to pass. (What is the difference between God's worldview of your life and the flesh's worldview? How can you gain God's perspective?)

- Free to express yourself in a world of contradictions. (What contradictions of life are you facing? How can you maintain your convictions in your actions and words with such an environment?)

- Free to look up and declare, 'The devil thought he had me, but God has set me free.' (Begin to declare this over and over until it sinks into your spirit.)"

## THINGS TO RESEARCH

1. Look up the following words in a standard dictionary and Bible dictionary, and find some verses that express their meaning. Then look at their causes and effects.

| RELEASED FROM THE BOX OF SINFUL FLESH | |
|---|---|
| BENEFITS | CAUSE AND EFFECTS |
| (No) Condemnation | |
| Redemption | |
| Justification | |
| Substitution | |
| Sanctification | |

- How does Jesus' death and resurrection entitle us to complete justification?

- How does His death and resurrection provide complete substitution?

- How does Christ bring us complete sanctification?

- How do these three benefits free us from our problems?

- How do they give us different solutions than we could find on our own?

- What did you discover that you did not know?

- What spoke to you during your research?

2. Look up the word *liberty* in a concordance and record key verses that describe our liberty in the Spirit of the Lord. How does the liberty that you receive cancel your slavery to the flesh?

## THINGS TO DO

1. Memorize Romans 8:1—*"There is therefore now no condemnation to those who are in Christ Jesus...."* Christ has done it, and you qualify for this complete removal of condemnation.

- If you are in Christ, when is it necessary for you to feel a little condemnation?

- Please explain if there should even be a shred of a teensy, weensy microscopic bit of condemnation for what you have done.

2. "Your action becomes the evidence of your faith." How do you need to act on your faith tomorrow?

- Is there a situation, relationship, or pattern that needs a strong application of faith?

- What will you do to act on your faith? Be sure to hold yourself accountable to follow through.

## THINGS TO PRAY

1. The authors say, "Your mind wants intimacy with God without the restriction of your flesh or your environment. Consequently, you will not be satisfied until you are released from the box of sinful flesh and your mind is connected to the Spirit of Christ."

- What does it take to achieve this type of intimacy?

- How can you practice this intimacy? Take time to do so.

2. "...it is through the Word that the Spirit of Christ releases all believers from bondage, while the flesh is fighting with the spirit."

- What do these words mean to you?

- If the Word of God is the key to unlocking your chains, you need to use it in prayer. Gather Scriptures that speak to any bondage or negative patterns that are holding you back from fulfilling your God-given purpose. Then pray these Scriptures in order to release God's will into your mind.

3.   Pray that God will show you your value in His eyes. "You are an original; and you cannot be duplicated, imitated, or destroyed." Allow the Lord to share why He made you as unique as you are. Take time to "look at the beautiful, powerful, joyful you—God's original and new creation."

## THINGS TO REACH FOR (Goals)

1.   Goal: Be all you can be. You may be saying, "I am not currently able to do all of the things I am capable of, but I want to reach my full potential. I want to be released from this box of sinful flesh so that I can be all that God has called me to be and achieve everything that God has placed in my mind."

- Do you know what God wants you to achieve and how to be in His will?

- Have you taken the first step toward this goal and understood your purpose on earth? If not, you need to clear up the debris that is keeping you from hearing His voice. If you have heard what God's purpose is for you, then you need to move forward.

- What steps do you need to continue to pursue your destiny? Is there training you need? Are there people you need to connect with? Do you have obstacles in your path that you must dig in and take care of?

- Whatever steps you can accomplish now or in the months ahead, write them down and place them on your list of to-dos.

2.   Goal: Personally maintain power over the flesh.

- What kind of process does it take to achieve such a goal?

- What are your weaknesses in the flesh?

- Have you tried to maintain control over them?

- How successful were you? What do you need to do in order to maintain power over your flesh?

- What role does your mind have in this?

- What verses of Scripture might you feed on to focus your mind away from the flesh and onto the Spirit in each of the weaknesses you listed? Make yourself a goal to use these Scriptures at appropriate times of temptation and weakness.

CHAPTER FIVE

# THEOLOGICAL AND PHILOSOPHICAL THOUGHTS AND CONCEPTS

Because of the nature of this chapter, we will address it differently than the others. Read the first section of Chapter Five—"The Mind Is the Seat of All Spiritual and Carnal Expressions" in *Battle for the Mind*.

## THINGS TO PONDER

1.   A theological view of the body and soul is that your body will die and then your soul will go to Heaven or hell.

   ▪ How would you explain the theological view of the body and soul?

   ▪ List three main concepts that clearly explain the difference between body and soul.

2.   Explain dualism and a brief history behind this philosophy. Underline any outstanding words or phrases under each of the philosophers/theologians in the "Philosophy" section.

   ▪ Read the second section of Chapter Five—"Word Wealth."

## THINGS TO RESEARCH

1.   Highlight anything that seems significant to you as you understand the nature of the words. Look up any Scriptures that are quoted, and read them in the context of the passage surrounding them.

   ▪ 1 Corinthians 1:12

   ▪ Romans 15:27

   ▪ John 5:24

   ▪ Romans 8:5

2.   Go through each of the "Use and Application" items at the end of each word entry. Why did the authors bring your attention to these? How do each of these principles set the standard for our thought processes and our actions?

* Read the next section of Chapter Five—"Practical Applications."

## THINGS TO REACH FOR (Goals)

Goal: Be able to apply your understanding of the theological and philosophical lessons learned in Chapters One through Five. Use this checklist to determine your progress. Circle each item as you evaluate where you are in the process.

Principle 1: "The mind is the seat of carnal and spiritual expressions, and you are to walk according to the Spirit."

* I understand this principle intellectually.

* I believe this principle and am ready to exercise the faith to operate in it.

* I am operating in the understanding of this principle.

* I am able to disciple someone else to walk in this principle.

Principle 2: "There is therefore now no condemnation," means Jesus not only paid the debt of sin, but also cleansed us from all unrighteousness.

* I understand this principle intellectually.

* I believe this principle and am ready to exercise the faith to operate in it.

* I am operating in the understanding of this principle.

* I am able to disciple someone else to walk in this principle.

## THINGS TO DO

Review the Memory Verses from Section One. Memorization should help you utilize these verses in the days and weeks to come.

* Romans 8:6

- Colossians 3:2

- Romans 8:7

- Proverbs 23:7

- Romans 8:1

The next section of Chapter Five, "Action Steps," is shown on the next page in an expanded form.

## THINGS TO PRAY AND LEARN

1.  "Seek God with all your heart and with all your soul." This may seem more like a goal than a prayer, but follow the steps outlined in *Battle for the Mind* and journal your experience beside each step.

| STEPS | YOUR THOUGHTS AND EXPERIENCES |
|---|---|
| Praise God for what He has already done. | |
| Meditate on what God is saying in Romans 8:1-13. Ask the Holy Spirit for guidance and understanding. | |
| Ask for what you want. Ask the Holy Spirit to reveal God's truth and will for you. | |
| Worship in Spirit and in truth. Commit to being transformed by the Word. | |
| Commit to spending at least 30 minutes a day with God only. | |
| Commit to fast and pray at least one day a week. | |
| End in thanksgiving and praise. | |

2.  "Begin each day in the reality that you are a new creature, that the Spirit of Christ dwells in you, and that you are no longer under condemnation for past sins."

- Make a card with the words, "I am a new creature. The Spirit of Christ dwells in me. I am no longer under condemnation for past sins." Put it on your bedside table and awaken to this truth every day.

- "Pray inwardly for the Lord to open your mind and understanding so you can learn the practical characteristics of a mind that is walking according to the Spirit and not according to the flesh." As you begin your study each day, open with this prayer so that you invite the Holy Spirit to be your teacher.

- "Spend time reading and studying God's Word." Every day you eat food for your body; you also need to eat food for your spirit. Commit to a reasonable, realistic amount of time. Make it easy enough that you know you can keep to it. Don't start with your ultimate goal; take the first steps toward that goal.

- "Prayerfully and carefully read John 14:17 to understand that when your mind is directed toward truth, you are aware that the Spirit of Christ dwells (lives) in you and that you are always in His presence." Does this realization make you feel special? Does it make you cringe with guilt? What should your reaction be?

- "Read Galatians 6:8 to understand how to please God by sowing seeds for the harvest." What seeds are you able to sow? Where is the fertile ground for sowing around you? What seeds should you sow through your words? What seeds should you sow through your life as a living witness?

- Sow the Word in order to win souls by sharing the Gospel and telling others of God's love, grace, and mercy. Note: living evangelistically is not only a privilege; it is rewarding. The following Scriptures are valuable tools for guiding others to salvation: John 3:16, Romans 10:9-10, and Acts 4:12." Look each of these Scriptures up and explain them as you would to an unbeliever. What are some of the "opening lines" you might use to share the Gospel with someone? What are some topics of discussion that would be easy for non-Christians to engage in, but that could lead to topics of spiritual truths?

Read the next section in Chapter Five—"Personal Growth and Development."

## THINGS TO DO

1. "The following Scriptures are valuable tools for understanding that love fulfills the law when you are walking according to the Spirit." Skim these passages briefly. You will use them again below.

- Romans 15:14
- 1 Corinthians 12:7-8
- Galatians 5:16-26
- John 15:2

2. "Pray and ask the Holy Spirit to lead you in prayer for guidance, repentance, and thanksgiving." As you gain a rhythm for your daily prayer times, utilize the ACTS acronym as a skeletal framework for your communion with God.

A=Adoration or honor for God

C=Confession of your sins

T=Thanksgiving and praise for what God has done

S=Supplication/Intercession (praying for the needs of others)

Read the next section in Chapter Five—"Read, Record, Reflect."

## THINGS TO LEARN

1. There are three bullet points that are helpful in gaining insight during Bible Study:

- "What does this passage say to me?
- Record you insights, notes, and questions.

- "Mark unfamiliar words or phrases." Research when needed through study helps or a learned person.

2.  Put these three into use for the following passages:

- Romans 15:14

- 1 Corinthians 12:7-8

- Galatians 5:16-26

- John 15:2

## THINGS TO REVIEW

Reread the introduction to Part One (before Chapter One). What summary statements can you give about what you have learned from this section?

PART TWO

# FINDING YOUR ORIGINAL SELF

Read the Introduction to Part Two in *Battle for the Mind*.

## THINGS TO PONDER

"Who am I?" Do your activities define who you are? (I am a golfer.) Do your roles define who you are? (I am a pastor's wife.) Do your relationships define who you are? (I am John's best friend.) Does your career define who you are? (I am Company X's cash accountant.) Where do these definitions lack clarity in describing the unique nature God has put within you? How does what you do come short of telling who you are on the inside?

## THINGS TO RESEARCH

Ask ten people to write five sentences about who you are. Don't give them any ideas as to what you are looking for. Just allow them to freely share what they think. Be sure to choose a wide variety of family, friends, and associates. After reading their responses, think about who you think you are and what other people see in you. Does your family tend to see you a certain way and your other associates in another way?

## THINGS TO PRAY

If you have never asked the question, "Who am I?" now is a great time to ask. Let the Lord describe you the way He sees you. Don't be afraid to receive positive affirmation from the Lord. Remember, He thought you were "very good" when He created you—in His image.

CHAPTER SIX

# I AM AN ORIGINAL

Read Chapter Six in *Battle for the Mind*.

## THINGS TO PONDER

1.   "There is no one like me in the whole wide world." It is easy to believe that, given the variety of physical and personality traits we see around us. You know Who made you so unique, but why did He do it? What purpose do you think your unique qualities have?

2.   "In the beginning of Romans chapter 12, Paul urges us to measure our lives to our belief."

- What are ten of your basic beliefs? List them.

How does your life measure to these beliefs?

- Is your life a testimony of your belief, or do others know what you believe by what you say and do?

3.   The authors give the illustration of how our lives can resemble either a pond or a river. Which body of water best describes your overall life at this time? Are there specific parts of your life that are more like the river analogy? What parts of your life seem to resemble a pond?

4.   "Anyone who is not renewing is dead, and dead things are completely controlled by the environment." Think about what this statement means to you.

- What importance does this principle put on renewing your mind?

- Does this need to be a moment-by-moment occurrence in order to stay alive?

5.   How does the Living Water flow from the Spirit of God into our spirits and minds and then to others and then begin the cycle all over again?

- Have you ever felt this transfer of life?

- How do you come to Christ and drink?

- How does He pour life back into you?

- How does this protect you against all the circumstances and environments that surround you?

## THINGS TO RESEARCH

1. In your understanding, what is the difference between a conformed mind (to copy) and a transformed mind (to create)? Think through the following Bible characters and give examples from their lives of how they demonstrated whether they were operating according to a conformed mind or a transformed mind.

| | DEMONSTRATED CONFORMED MIND | DEMONSTRATED TRANSFORMED MIND |
|---|---|---|
| Abraham | *When he told Pharaoh that Sarah was his sister* | *When he was ready to sacrifice Isaac on the altar* |
| Jacob | | |
| Moses | | |
| Miriam | | |
| David | | |
| Peter | | |
| Paul | | |

2. "Because you are now connected to the Spirit of Christ, the Living Water, your mind is being renewed and refreshed with the original and creative breath or wind from the Holy Spirit of God." Use a concordance and look up references to *Living Water* in the Bible.

- Which references give hope to the people who receive the Living Water?

- How do these references show the change that can take place in a person's life?

## THINGS TO DO

Memorize Romans 12:2—*"And be not conformed to this world: but be ye transformed by the renewing of your mind, that ye may prove what is that good, and acceptable, and perfect will of God"* (KJV). As Christians, we desire to live in God's will. Here is the key—renew your mind! Try to catch yourself when old thought patterns emerge, and stop them in their neurological tracks! Go for the good and the acceptable and the perfect!

## THINGS TO PRAY

1. You need to be personally connected to the Holy Spirit, who is the life source for your mind. Become a pursuer of the Holy Spirit and pray that the Counselor will open the floodgates so that faith will flow into your spirit and mind.

2. Have you ever wanted to be (conform) like someone else so much so that you wished you had what they had (talents, abilities, circumstances, wealth, and so forth)? If so,

- Take time to confess that you have substituted a mere person's nature for God's preferred nature that He placed within you. Repent of your shortsightedness.

- Ask the Lord to forgive you and release you from the burden of needing to be like someone else. Accept His full pardon and the liberty He gives. Remember, when you conform, you are denying the creative purpose that God has for you.

## THINGS TO REACH FOR (Goals)

Goal: Use this week to take steps to allow your spirit to flow with the Holy Spirit. Each day affirm that you want your mind to be your inner self, your heart, your soul, your appetite, your total person...who you are. Pray that the Spirit of God will spawn creativity in your mind. Keep a journal available to jot down ideas and thoughts as they come into your mind during this week. They may seem random, but at the end of the week, look to see if they may just be the creative work of the Holy Spirit transforming your mind.

CHAPTER SEVEN

# HOW TO CHANGE YOURSELF

Read Chapter Seven in *Battle for the Mind*.

## THINGS TO PONDER

1. "Now that you are transformed and have a new mind, you can dictate to your environment."

- What does this mean to you?

- Do you think you have dominion over your environment? Does this include people? Why or why not?

2. Aristotle defined change as "the passage from potentiality to actuality."

According to what the authors have shared so far in this book, what do you think will make the change in your ability to see your potential come to actual fulfillment?

- What potential do you see in yourself that has yet to be fulfilled?

- What kind of outside pressure or external force needs to be applied for change to occur?

- "Change can be temporary." What are some examples of where you have changed your thinking for a time, but came back to your original way of thinking?

- "Change can also be long-term or permanent." What are some examples of internal changes that lasted over a long period of time?

- How is being transformed by the renewal of your mind a permanent change? Why does this renewal demand that you stay connected to the Spirit of Christ?

3. "With your transformed mind you can now expect to win all the battles in your mind..."? The word *all* is an extreme word to use. What do you think the about this concept:

- Why is it used here?

- Can you believe this to be true?

- Do you have the faith to exercise this belief in your daily life?

4. Why is it so critical for you to understand how faith and reason work together?

- Is there a conflict between faith and reason?

- Why does the world seem to think so?

- How do these help us to live our lives according to the Spirit and to be conformed to the world?

## THINGS TO RESEARCH

1. The authors tell us that if we want transformation to take place, a change must occur. They give some meanings of the word *change*. Research the scope of this word. Look it up in a standard dictionary and in a Bible dictionary.

- What does the apostle Paul say about change?

- Think about the life of Moses; what kinds of changes occurred in his life that transformed him?

- How does someone change from being carnal to being spiritual?

- How does the Spirit of Christ give the power to effect change?

2. "God is now your material and spiritual source of life." Review the following biblical characters and relate how they experienced God's provision both materially and spiritually.

| BIBLICAL CHARACTER | EVIDENCE OF GOD'S PROVISION (SCRIPTURE REFERENCES) |
|---|---|
| Daniel | |
| Nehemiah | |
| Cornelius | |
| The disciples | |
| Ruth | |

3. Take a survey from those who see or speak to you on a daily basis. Give them a paper that has the fruit of the Spirit written on it. Have them evaluate the evidence of these fruit thus far in your life on a scale of 1-10. Let them be anonymous so that they can share freely.

| EVALUATE EVIDENCE OF THE FRUIT OF THE SPIRIT | 1 | 2 | 3 | 4 | 5 | 6 | 7 | 8 | 9 | 10 |
|---|---|---|---|---|---|---|---|---|---|---|
| Love | | | | | | | | | | |
| Joy | | | | | | | | | | |
| Peace | | | | | | | | | | |
| Long-suffering | | | | | | | | | | |
| Kindness | | | | | | | | | | |
| Goodness | | | | | | | | | | |
| Faithfulness | | | | | | | | | | |
| Gentleness | | | | | | | | | | |
| Self-control | | | | | | | | | | |

- What is your "top fruit"?
- Do certain fruit seem to shine in different circumstances or with different people?
- Where do you need to be transformed the most?

## THINGS TO DO

1.   The authors ask this question: "Have you ever felt trapped in a situation, somewhere you did not want to be, and then all of a sudden you broke free by the power of your own intuition, by the power of your connection with God?"

- Have you experienced this? If so, explain.

- When you finally feel the liberation, what do you do?

- How do you express yourself?

If you are like most and have many of these experiences, they are testimonies that can help others see the liberating power of God. Tuck them into your evangelism log as "conversation starters" for when you see someone else looking trapped. Then you can gently speak words of identification with them and later add the hope that you experienced.

2.   Memorize Romans 8:2—*"For the law of the Spirit of life in Christ Jesus has made me free from the law of sin and death."* What is the difference between these two laws?

3.   The quote from John Calvin includes these words, "...God Himself has implanted in all men a certain understanding of His divine majesty." Read Romans chapter 1 to determine the verses that show the basis for Calvin's statement. Since God has made Himself plainly visible internally and externally, are unbelievers in denial?

## THINGS TO PRAY

1.   Take time to allow the Holy Spirit to let you see the path before you and what steps you are to take next in terms of your closest relationships, your career, your ministry, and your long-term goals. Pray that He brings your potential forward so that you can pursue it. Praise God that you are a "new and original creation."

- How does a Christian "walk according to the Spirit"?

- How does the Holy Spirit "constantly transform and renew you"?

2. "You no longer want to live according to the desires of the flesh and the dictates of the world." Is this statement true of you? Are there fleshly desires that encumber you?

- Open your heart to the Lord, and ask His searchlight to examine the corners of your mind, showing any hidden obstacles that hinder this attitude from coming to pass in your life.

## THINGS TO REACH FOR (Goals)

Goal: Renew yourself constantly. The authors tell us, "Renew yourself constantly, because renewal is a part of the life process." How does this renewal take place in the mind (spirit)? Should this renewal be consistent? Should it take place weekly? Daily? Hourly?

As you leave for work or school each day, ask the Holy Spirit to regenerate your body and mind with the Living Water. Ask Him to establish an "atmosphere in you that does not have anything to do with the atmosphere outside." During your day, remind yourself to drink in the Living Water again.

CHAPTER EIGHT

# THE MASQUERADE IS OVER!

Read Chapter Eight of *Battle for the Mind*.

## THINGS TO PONDER

1. "It is quite evident that our environment teaches us to act like others around us." What actions do you emulate from those around you?

- How has your environment influenced your personality development for the good?

- How has environment embedded habits of evil?

- How does manipulation work to keep you from being transformed?

- Have you ever felt that someone was manipulating you away from the Living Water?

- How can you identify manipulation and be immune to its bombardment of your thoughts, concepts, and desires?

2. Have you ever been "in the middle of a battle and you said something that was completely out of character for you"? Or have you ever been "involved in a relationship where you acted in ways that you didn't even know yourself"?

- In these incidents, how did you take on an "outward expression that did not come from the inside of you"?

- How can you avoid such behavior in the future?

3. "When God places something in your mind, it takes time for the environment to adjust to who you are." Why does it take time for people to adjust to the "new" you?

- What fruit of the Spirit do you need in order to go through the time needed for your environment to make the adjustment?

## THINGS TO RESEARCH

1.   Research the word *conform*. First, write down the origins of the word as described in the book. Then look it up in a standard dictionary and in a Bible dictionary. Using a concordance, look up Scriptures that describe what things we should and should not conform to.

2.   The authors highlight how David fought Goliath using what he knew to be his strengths and not conforming to Saul's strengths. Research other people from the Scripture who remained connected to God and did not conform to what the world was offering. Do you identify with any of these people or their problems?

3.   Look up the word *transfigured* in a standard dictionary and a Bible dictionary. How does this word apply to how your mind is to be transformed?

## THINGS TO DO

1.   "As an original, living with a renewed mind, you are no longer a clone of anyone else." This is an important principle that you must embrace to move forward. Write these words somewhere that you can see them every day this week and say them aloud. Allow the Lord to make you aware of when others are influencing you in a negative way.

2.   Memorize Second Corinthians 3:18: *"But we all, with unveiled face, beholding as in a mirror the glory of the Lord, are being transformed into the same image from glory to glory, just as by the Spirit of the Lord."* Remind yourself that you are being changed in steps and are moving on in glory.

## THINGS TO PRAY

Read Jeremiah 2:13: *"For My people have committed two evils: They have forsaken Me, the fountain of living waters, and hewn themselves cisterns— broken cisterns that can hold no water."*

- Since God is the "fountain of living water," what are the "cisterns" that we fashion?

- Why don't these hold water? Take time before the Lord to identify the cisterns that you have hewn out and break them as an act of contrition. Confess, repent, and then be cleansed and healed!

## THINGS TO REACH FOR (Goals)

Goal: Be in control of your own mind. "If you are not in control of your own mind, you are being controlled." Take steps necessary to increase your control over your mind. After you have completed the questions and prayer times above, keep track in your journal as to how you are doing each day for a month. Every night, write down any incident that shows whether you are succumbing to another's control or whether you successfully remained in control.

CHAPTER NINE

# THE POWER OF A RENEWED MIND

Read Chapter Nine in *Battle for the Mind*.

## THINGS TO PONDER

1.   The authors tell us that when we are renewed through our connection with the Holy Spirit, the mind is set on a higher level.

- What does this mean to you?
- How do you know that the level is higher than what your mind was before you were renewed?
- What patterns of thought are present that were not there before?
- What thought patterns are absent because your mind has been renewed?

2.   "You are in control of your mind." Do you feel like you are in control of your mind today? Why or why not?

- How do you know when you are in control?
- What characteristics show you that renewal has taken place?
- What victory is still awaiting you?
- What power do you need to see?
- Where is joy absent?
- How does your daily walk "in the world, but not of the world" become a part of your journey to higher heights?

3.   "Satan can no longer control you because the fountain of Living Water is so far down in you that the devil cannot reach it." How does this work for a Christian? Where is the place that the devil cannot reach?

## THINGS TO RESEARCH

1. "Scripture records Jesus boldly saying, 'I AM the Truth; I AM the Light; I AM the Vine. I AM, I AM, I AM.' The 'I AMness' separates Him from everyone else." Use your concordance and look up some references to *I AM,* both from the Old Testament and the New Testament. Be sure to include Moses at the burning bush and the letters to the churches in Revelation. How is God (Jesus/Holy Spirit) unique from anyone else? How is He one-of-a-kind?

2. Jesus said that He had come to give us abundant life. Look up the word *abundant* in a standard dictionary and a Bible dictionary. How is abundance given to us materially? Physically? Emotionally? Mentally? Spiritually?

## THINGS TO DO

Memorize Isaiah 26:3—*"You will keep him in perfect peace whose mind is stayed on You...."*

- What does "perfect peace" mean to you?
- How does this peace fit into the abundant life that Jesus spoke of in John 10:10?

## THINGS TO PRAY

1. Take the expressions of I AM that you researched and have a time of praise. Include these I AMs to let the Lord God know His worth in your eyes. Assign Him the glory, honor, thanks, power, and strength that are due His name.

2. "When you have the mind of Christ, you will step into your 'I AMness.'" Begin to boldly pray your "I AMness." Elaborate on the benefits you receive from each characteristic. Thank God for allowing you to be made in His likeness (I AMness).

- I am released from satan and his demons.
- I am going to be what God created me to be.

- I am growing by the power of God, and the real me is about to be released.

- I am totally original, I am not a copy, and I cannot be duplicated.

- I am winning this mind game because God put winning in my spirit.

- I am going to overcome.

- I am an original blessing from God.

- I am going to stand up and claim what is mine.

## THINGS TO REACH FOR (Goals)

Goal: To win the game in your mind. The authors tell us that we can boldly say, "I am expected to win the mind games; I am running with all my heart, and I am going to overcome and win because God put winning in my mind."

- Do you really expect to win the mind games satan plays with you?

- How can you build up your faith over this week so you will expect to win to a greater degree than you currently are? Check at the end of the week to see how much your expectation has increased.

CHAPTER TEN

# THEOLOGICAL AND PHILOSOPHICAL THOUGHTS AND CONCEPTS

Read the first section of Chapter Ten in *Battle for the Mind*

## THINGS TO PONDER

1.  Read Chapter Ten and explain three theological views of why we perceive God by faith and not by reason. What role does reason have in our relationship with God?

2.  Explain "reasons for faith" and write a summary of what was said under this column. Underline any outstanding words or phrases under each of the philosophers/theologians in the "Philosophy" section.

Read the second section of Chapter Ten—"Word Wealth."

## THINGS TO RESEARCH

1.  Highlight anything that seems significant to you as you understand the nature of the words. Look up any Scriptures that are quoted and read them in the context of the passage surrounding them.

- 2 Corinthians 1:3
- Romans 12:1
- Isaiah 54:8,10
- Romans 6:13
- Romans 12:2

2.  Go through each of the "Use and Application" items at the end of each word entry. Why did the authors bring your attention to these? How does each of these principles set the standard for our thought processes and our actions?

Read the next section of Chapter Ten—"Practical Applications."

## THINGS TO REACH FOR (Goals)

Goal: Be able to apply your understanding of the theological and philosophical lessons learned in Chapters Six through Ten. Use this checklist to determine your progress. Circle each item as you evaluate where you are in the process.

Principle 1: "Your connection to God is based on faith and not reason."

- I understand this principle intellectually.

- I believe this principle and am ready to exercise the faith to operate in it.

- I am operating in the understanding of this principle.

- I am able to disciple someone else to walk in this principle.

Principle 2: "The conflict is not between faith and reason, but between faith and sight."

- I understand this principle intellectually.

- I believe this principle and am ready to exercise the faith to operate in it.

- I am operating in the understanding of this principle.

- I am able to disciple someone else to walk in this principle.

Principle 3: "Transformation takes place in the mind."

- I understand this principle intellectually.

- I believe this principle and am ready to exercise the faith to operate in it.

- I am operating in the understanding of this principle.

- I am able to disciple someone else to walk in this principle.

The next section of Chapter Ten, "Action Steps," is shown below in an expanded form.

| ACTION STEPS | YOUR THOUGHTS AND EXPERIENCES |
|---|---|
| Praise God for what He has already done | |
| Meditate on what God is saying in Romans 8:1-13. Ask The Holy Spirit for guidance and understanding. | |
| Ask for what you want. Ask the Holy Spirit to reveal God's truth and will for you. | |
| Worship in Spirit and in truth. Commit to being transformed by the Word. | |
| Commit to spend at least 30 minutes a day with God only. | |
| Commit to fast and pray at least one day a week. | |
| End in thanksgiving and praise. | |

## THINGS TO DO

1.   Review the Memory Verses from Section Two. Memorization should help you utilize these verses in the days and weeks to come.

- Romans 12:2

- Romans 8:2

- 2 Corinthians 3:18

- Isaiah 26:3

2.   Read and memorize Mark 12:29-31 and First Peter 3:15.

*The most important one, answered Jesus, is this: Hear, O Israel, the Lord our God, the Lord is one. Love the Lord your God with all your heart and with all your soul and with all your mind and with all your strength. The second is this: Love your neighbor as yourself. There is no commandment greater than these* (Mark 12:29-31 NIV).

*But in your hearts revere Christ as Lord. Always be prepared to give an answer to everyone who asks you to give the reason for the hope that you have. But do this with gentleness and respect* (First Peter 3:15 NIV).

Be prepared to explain these verses, demonstrating how God has given you a mind and expects you to use it.

## THINGS TO PRAY AND LEARN

1. "Prayerfully and carefully read Romans 12:1-2 and Hebrews 10:19-25." As you pray these verses, ask the Holy Spirit to reveal what actions you might take that will let God's Word and the Spirit of God maintain control of your transformed and renewed mind.

2. "Show that you have faith by believing in God's promises, because God will do what He says He will do":

- "Celebrate daily that you have gained access to God through the shed blood of Jesus Christ. Tell others what God has done or is doing in your life, and give thanks to God for everything—even the small things." Ask someone to be your "celebration partner" for this week. Talk to this person daily about what you have to celebrate.

- "Have complete confidence and belief in God. Let the Word shape your thinking. Apply God's Word directly to your situations—insert your name in the text as you read the Scripture and let the Word speak directly to you and your specific situations and issues." If you have a reading plan all ready in place, just continue following it and use these ideas to personalize your study. If you are not currently studying the Word daily, begin reading a Psalm, a chapter from the Old Testament, and a chapter from the New Testament each day. Apply the ideas suggested here to make these Scriptures yours.

- "Do not worry. Pray and trust God; He will fulfill His promises, even when you don't see any evidence." How easily do you fall into the trap of worry? Are there certain aspects of life where you are most vulnerable to becoming anxious or worrisome? Identifying the traps is the first step toward transforming your mind. Pray for trust. Find a promise from God's Word that speaks to your area of concern or challenge and pray the promise through until you believe it.

- "Seek God diligently through prayer and meditation, and believe that He will reward you for it." What rewards can you expect from seeking God? Read Deuteronomy 4:29, First Chronicles 16:10, Second Chronicles 7:14, Psalm 22:26, and Psalm 27:4 (and any others you would like).

- "Practice persistent and patient praise." What is "persistent" praise? Does this mean we are to praise even when we don't feel like it? Does this mean we are to praise consistently? What is "patient" praise? Does this mean we are to increase our praise time beyond what our physical bodies can endure? Pursue these characteristics and see how your praise life changes.

- "Sing a hymn or song that reminds you to trust and praise Him for guiding you: *You are to continually offer the sacrifice of praise to God, which is the fruit of your lips giving thanks to His name*' (see Heb. 13:15)." Pick a "song of the day" that you will hum or sing repeatedly to remind you of the trust relationship you have with your Guide.

- "Read First Peter 2:5 to understand that by the renewing of your mind, your body is now a temple—a spiritual house, a thank-offering to God." You have been focusing on renewing your mind. How does your body line up with that renewal? How do you become a thank-offering to God?

- "Read Romans 13:21 to understand that with your new mind, your relationship to the world has changed." Can you catalog the changes that have taken place so far through this study? How has your mind changed? How has your relationship to the world changed?

- "Behave like a Christian in every part of your life—job, activities, recreation, attitudes, giving, shopping, dancing, eating, talking." This may seem like an impossible goal, but as your mind is renewed, these will become easier. Which of these parts of your life is the easiest place to act like a Christian? Which is the most difficult? What should you do to commit all of these areas to the Lord?

Read the next section in Chapter Ten—"Personal Growth and Development."

## THINGS TO DO

Some of these items have been covered under other sections. However, we will list the rest here. We have amplified and highlighted certain ones for your continued growth.

- "Spend daily time with God through the Word."

- "Pray and meditate upon God's Word that your basic thinking patterns are being changed." How does God's Word change someone's thinking patterns? How do you meditate or pray God's Word?

- "Seek God's will so that you know what He wants, and then do what is good and pleasing to God." Practice listening as much as talking when you pray.

- "You are called to a different lifestyle than what the world offers with its behaviors and customs. You are now living according to the essential nature of the spiritual mind; hence, you are now required to:

- "Love without hypocrisy." No gossip, even for the most "innocent" of reasons.

- "Abhor what is evil." How much do you hate evil? Does it show to others around you?

- "Cling to what is good." How much do you love righteousness?

- "Be kind and affectionate to one another." This includes even the people who irritate you the most.

- "Serve the Lord." This may seem simplistic, but do you really know that what you are currently doing is where God would have you serve? Don't serve people or merely meet their expectations; do what God wants.

- "Rejoice in hope and be patient in tribulation." Do people see you as a person of hope? This is beyond being a positive person. This is looking at the unseen realm from God's perspective. How patient are you when things go wrong? Are you more patient with people or with things? What is God's reward for patience?

- "Pray continually." This means that you are to get up praying and to keep on praying until you sleep. Though you will do hundreds of tasks during the day, you are to be in a constant state of prayer so that all is given to the Lord.

- "Give to the needs of others." Think of someone who needs something that you have and give it away.

- "Live peacefully with others." There are some people who seem to know what button to push. The next time they push your button, pretend that the button didn't work. Breathe in the Holy Spirit, and breathe out peace. Remember, a soft answer turns away wrath.

- "Love your enemy." Believe it or not, there are some people who will never like you. These people may even cause you problems on purpose. Yet how did Jesus treat Judas, His close friend who purposefully betrayed Him? Unlike Jesus, your betrayal is, most likely, not a matter of life and death, so you should be able to choose to love your enemy.

- "Memorize verses from the Scriptures so that you are always ready to give a testimony and a defense to everyone who asks for the reason you have hope (faith) in God."

■ "Believe that Jesus is Lord, so you can say, as C.S. Lewis said, 'I believe in Christianity as I believe that the sun has risen; not only because I see it, but because by it I see everything else.'"

## THINGS TO REVIEW

Reread the chapter titles and section titles in Chapters Six through Nine. What summary statements can you give about what you have learned from this Section?

SECTION TWO

# ENJOYING FREEDOM IN CHRIST

Read Section Two in *Battle for the Mind*.

## THINGS TO PONDER

1. "Freedom is critical to experiencing the kind of life that God has always intended for you." Why is this true?

   ▪ How does freedom make the difference? Freedom from what things? Freedom for what things?

2. "Jesus came to reverse the natural order that exists in both the secular and the spiritual world...His way to freedom is...different...the last is first, the least is greatest, and the humble finds grace."

   ▪ Contrast what the world believes about freedom with what Jesus' viewpoint is.

   ▪ How does humility fit into this picture?

## THINGS TO RESEARCH

Ask the following teaser question to some non-Christians that you see this week: "What do you think *freedom* is?" After listening carefully to their responses, ask them the following question, rephrasing it with some of the words from their answer: "So, if you _____ (their answer) _____, then you would know freedom?"

   ▪ Depending upon how the conversation is going, you could ask, "Is every person's idea of freedom the same?" From your conversations, analyze what people think of freedom and how personal they make their definitions.

- Also, compare and contrast their answers with the principle in John 8:32 that tells us that freedom is predisposed to the truth. Would these people be able to handle the truth that God offers us?

## THINGS TO DO

Memorize John 8:32—*"And you shall know the truth, and the truth shall make you free."* The world often questions God's truth and purports to host its own truth. How do you know what is true? How can you be sure of the truth?

## THINGS TO PRAY

Ask God to prepare your heart for His truth so you can experience His freedom in a greater dimension.

INTRODUCTION

# A NEW MODEL FOR THE MIND—TRUTH FROM THE BOOK OF PHILIPPIANS

Read the Introduction to Section Two in *Battle for the Mind*.

## THINGS TO PONDER

1.  The Book of Philippians "provides practical application for thanksgiving, rejoicing, and praising the Lord in the midst of adverse circumstances." Where do you need this practical application in your life today? What adverse circumstance (no matter how large or how small) is robbing you of praise and rejoicing?

2.  What does it mean to have "the same mind (or attitude)" as Christ?

   ▪ How do you exemplify Christ's attitude in your daily walk?

   ▪ Where do you need an attitude adjustment?

3.  "When you have the mind of Christ, you can face anything simply because of the strength of your mind." Why is this true?

   ▪ How is it possible?

   ▪ What is necessary for such an outcome?

## THINGS TO RESEARCH

1.  Read Philippians chapters 2 and 4. Search for verses that fall under the following categories:

   ▪ Verses of rejoicing

   ▪ Verses of giving God accolades or praise

   ▪ Verses of love and thanks

   ▪ Verses of exhortation

2. "Paul was obviously so deeply rooted in God that, no matter what was happening in his life, he kept his mind on Christ Jesus." Do you know someone whose mind is focused on the Lord in the same way as Paul's was?

- Ask that how he or she maintains such a steadfast focus.

- What keeps this person from falling back into a worldly mind-set?

## THINGS TO DO

1. Skim the entire Book of Philippians to prepare for the next chapters of the book. As you do, highlight any verses that speak to your heart or current situations. Make note of anything that you need to look up for further research. Star anything that seems new to you. Make a list of the verses that speak to the all-sufficiency of Christ.

2. Interview two or three Christians you know and ask them to tell you a story of how God has been all-sufficient to them.

- Note the mind or attitude they have as they share.

- Are there any similarities between the stories?

- What underlying principles come through each testimony?

## THINGS TO PRAY

1. Ask the Lord to help you receive true joy. Ask Him to put within you the instructions He gave to the Church about humility, leadership, servanthood, and greatness. Pray through the acrostic for JOY:

J = Jesus

O = Others

Y = You

2. Ask God to exchange any depression you have for perseverance and strength. Ask God to build you up so that when the next trial and tribulation comes, you will be ready to serve God so vehemently that your living witness will show forth.

3.  Focus on the I AM who is the Most High God. Speak these things about the Lord each day this week in your prayer time to build your faith:

- I AM enough when you have nothing.

- I AM enough to heal you.

- I AM enough to deliver you.

- I AM enough when everyone is against you.

- I AM enough when you don't have money.

- I AM enough for whatever you need.

## THINGS TO REACH FOR (Goals)

Goal: To live is Christ; to die is gain. Meditate on Philippians 1:21: *"For me, to live is Christ, and to die is gain."* To gain this attitude means that you must believe that your "circumstances should never dictate the quality of your relationship with God; you are to praise God at all times." Now, meditate on Psalm 34:1: *"I will bless the Lord at all times; His praise shall continually be in my mouth."* As you set the goal to see that your life is in Christ, you will need to control your mind and, therefore, your mouth. Every time a challenge or problem comes your way this week, write down the challenge on a piece of paper, using a couple of words (i.e. boss didn't like my report). Then begin to bless God in your mind and form praise words in your mouth. By the end of the week, see what progress you may have made toward living for Christ.

PART THREE

# A NEW MIND

Read the Introduction to Part Three in *Battle for the Mind*.

## THINGS TO PONDER

"Your thinking determines your actions. Negative thinking will enslave you and steal your freedom."

- How has your mind-set determined your actions?
- Have you had a time when negative thinking began to enslave you and steal your freedom?
- From what you have learned thus far, how can you become a positive thinker?

## THINGS TO PRAY

The authors tell us that because of the corruption your mind has experienced, you don't "need just a little change here and there;" your mind needs "a total change." You have learned that this change is a process. When you see some victory in your life, you cannot stop there. You must see things through until the end. Continue working on transforming your mind by praying through the following:

1. Confess your sin openly. Let your heart be vulnerable to the Lord. Ask the Lord to shine His searchlight and expose any unconfessed or hidden sin. Repent and turn from those specific areas that the Lord has revealed.

2. Confess any negativity that you have harbored in your mind. Ask the Holy Spirit to invade your thought life with those things that are honorable and worthy of praise.

3. Forgive those people who have rejected you. Set your will to release them from any debt you think they owe to you. Let the Holy Spirit pull any leftover anger or any root of bitterness out of your heart so that you can not only forgive, but also clear your mind of the situation or relationship struggle.

CHAPTER ELEVEN

# ACHIEVING UNITY THROUGH HUMILITY

Read Chapter Eleven in *Battle for the Mind*.

## THINGS TO PONDER

1. "In chapter 2 of Philippians, Paul presents a case for unity to the people of the church in Philippi. Paul declares that in order to gain unity, there must be humility." Why is this true?

- Is unity achieved by a merging of differences? Why or why not?

- Is unity achieved through deferring to one another? Why or why not?

- How do most Christians find humility?

2. The authors make a case for changing the translation of Philippians 2:1. Read aloud the standard translation and their new version—by changing each *if* to *because,* which they propose is closer to the meaning of the original Greek words.

- What does the new version mean to you?

- How is our unity with Christ the groundwork for our unity with other people?

3. The authors tell us, "It will bring great joy when the members (of the Church) are thinking the same thoughts—to love one another, to be like-minded, having the same love, and being of one accord."

- Do you think that you will truly see this in your lifetime?

- Does "thinking the same thoughts" mean that we are clones of one another? Explain this phrase to your understanding.

4. "When people act as individuals in a collective environment, it creates problems, defeating teamwork and effective group participation."

- When have you seen this style of "ministry" take place?
- How can it hurt the working ministries of the Church?
- How can it create discord among people who seem to be wonderful Christians?

5. What is the "fellowship of the Spirit"?

- How does the power of God move when this fellowship exists?
- Have you experienced this type of fellowship?
- What does it take to see this commonality come to pass?

## THINGS TO RESEARCH

1. Paul tells us to be *"like-minded."* The authors give us some background for this word in the Hebrew and Greek. Read through this again and catch the significance of this word. Now look it up in a dictionary and in a Bible dictionary. Are there other places where this word is used in the Bible?

2. Paul also tells us to be of *"one accord."* Look this phrase up in a concordance and find other verses that describe the behaviors, situations, and other results that come from being in one accord. Who are the people or organizations with which you feel you are in one accord? Are these relationships hallmarked by the same results you found in your research?

3. Do a word study on *humility*. Search the definition from a standard dictionary and also a Bible concordance. Look for examples of humility in the Bible and some verses to apply to your own life.

## THINGS TO DO

1. Memorize Romans 15:5-6: *"Now may the God of patience and comfort grant you to be like-minded toward one another, according to Christ Jesus, that you may with one mind, and one mouth glorify the God and Father of our Lord Jesus Christ."* This sounds right to most of us. Why don't we see more of this in the Body of Christ?

- What is the missing ingredient?

- How can you make a difference in the circle of people within your influence?

2.  It may be easy for you to love someone who is very compatible in personality to your personality or to honor someone who you look up to. But how hard is it for you to love someone who is not in one accord with you? Think of a person whom you feel out of sync with or a relationship that is troubling to you. Commit yourself to show love to that person, even if that person does not show appreciation for your love or a change in behavior toward you in any way. Choose to love because God said so and because it glorifies Him, making way for unity.

3.  The authors tell us that philosophers agree "that nothing is more rare than lowliness of mind." Why do you think this is true? From the philosopher quotes cited in the book, how does lowliness make love possible?

4.  If you live with family members, call a meeting to discuss how you can work through storms of life by meeting together and not judging each other, but touching and agreeing for the best in the name of Jesus. Allow every family member the privilege of assembling the family for such a meeting. Encourage each person to use this method or procedure for family unity. You may need to be the first in order to start the process!

## THINGS TO PRAY

1.  Ask the Lord to help you turn away from any selfish ambition or conceited attitudes you may have. Remember, you may not realize these on your own; they could be blind spots in your personality. And satan likes to deceive you into thinking that you really don't have problems with these issues. Therefore, you must wait before the Lord and let the Holy Spirit bring to mind anything that causes you to lift yourself up in front of someone else. Also, ask Him to show you where you think more highly of yourself than you ought, especially in terms of any expectations you have or rights you may think belong to you.

2.  Ask the Lord to allow your heart "to be tender and sympathetic at all times." A lack of tenderness and sympathy can often be seen when you

judge other people's actions or jump to "logical" conclusions about why they do what they do. Be sure to only let the Lord reveal what He thinks about others and turn off your worldly mind-set toward others. Pray this through until you feel that the Lord has given you a breakthrough in any negative habits you have toward others.

3. The authors tell us that the Church "has become a battleground of conflict that has nothing to do with the Gospel." What do you think they mean by this? What battles have you seen or experienced? Begin praying for Church leadership, starting with your church and going through national church leaders. Ask God to keep them true to the Gospel and open to embracing others. Ask God to give wisdom to leaders so that they might handle disagreements with godly wisdom and not worldly tenets.

4. "It's not by virtue of the indwelling of the Holy Spirit; it's by virtue of His control of your life. Yes, you can be indwelled by the Holy Spirit a long time before the Spirit has control over you." Pray that the Holy Spirit will continue to gain control. Lift up any areas you are aware of that need His control.

## THINGS TO REACH FOR (Goals)

Goal: Live together in love. "It is through the love of Jesus Christ that our souls are united, our hearts are in unison, and we can truly live together in love as though we have one mind and one spirit between us." Think through your close relationships. Choose one that can grow into this type of love if you commit yourselves to spending the time together to achieve it and choose to be bonded by something higher than your earthly relationship. Track your relationship over the next month and see how you are doing in terms of your Christ-like love.

CHAPTER TWELVE

# EXCHANGING YOUR MIND FOR GOD'S MIND

Read Chapter Twelve in *Battle for the Mind*.

## THINGS TO PONDER

1.  "With the mind of Christ, you should be willing to adopt Christ's attitude of love, unselfishness, servanthood, humility, and obedience, looking beyond your own interest for the sake of others." Does *willing* mean that even if you adopt this attitude grudgingly, you have still fulfilled it by exercising your will? To what extent are you willing to show the attitude of Christ? Will it sometimes be merely an act of obedience? Will it sometimes be a delight to have this attitude? Is there anything you know that makes the difference between these two poles of the spectrum?

- Why is humility not a problem when you love?

- What makes an act of humility become a demonstration of love?

- How are these acts a witness to others of how Christ is changing us?

2.  Jesus did not "unlawfully seize" His deity to do the work that was required of Him.

- How can you sometimes "unlawfully seize" your gifts, talents, experience, education, or status and use them for your own purposes?

- How can you acknowledge your gifts and such while still living humbly?

## THINGS TO RESEARCH

1.  "Listening to other people who want to tell you what you should or should not do can destroy your relationship and fellowship with the ones

you love." Take a survey among some of your closest associates. Be sure to have some Christians and some non-Christians in your survey, and ask them the following questions:

- Have you have ever experienced a time when someone's well-meaning advice actually caused more problems rather than solving them?

- Will you still ask that person who gave the bad counsel to continue to give advice or direction?

- Do you have others you receive counsel from?

- How did you choose these people?

2.   Read Daniel 10:8-15. Note the different ranks of the angels.

- What levels of power did each angel have?

- If we were to see such power demonstrated, what would most of the world think?

- Since God's power is far beyond any angel's power, what types of things could Jesus have done with His power that He chose not to do? Think about the temptations in the desert and those who misunderstood Him in order to complete your answer.

## THINGS TO DO

1.   Memorize Philippians 2:5: *"Let this mind be in you which was also in Christ Jesus."* Use this verse to remind you not only of the attitude of humility that Christ bore for your sake, but also of your need to embrace His attitude in your mind with enthusiasm.

2.   "Serving someone else doesn't make you less of a person; it actually makes you better." Pick an unlikely person to serve today. Make it an act of love and humility in a way that will catch this person off guard, but that this person will surely enjoy. Do not hold expectations of gratitude for your act. Simply do it as unto the Lord. "Remember, when you humble yourself, the Lord shall raise you up."

3.   Reread the section of Chapter Twelve titled, "Jesus—In the Form of God." As you read, highlight sentences that you need to remember that would help you explain this doctrine to someone else. You should use your own words, but be able to talk about the concepts in brief. This is a good exercise to have ready when you speak with someone who recognizes Jesus as a good "person," but does not understand or accept His deity.

## THINGS TO PRAY

1.   "There is more to Christ Jesus than His form and expression—Jesus Christ is Lord." Think about the ways in which Jesus is Lord: in the world around you, in those with whom you have close relationships, and within yourself. Have you locked Him out of any areas of your life so that He is not Lord? If so, confess these before the Lord of all and repent. Allow the Lord Jesus to take His rightful place on the throne in your heart.

2.   Using your Bible, pray Philippians 2:1-11 each day this week. To personalize it, use your name or the personal pronouns *I* and *me* to fit in wherever appropriate. Before you pray, ask the Holy Spirit to help you "have this mind which was in Christ Jesus."

## THINGS TO REACH FOR (Goals)

Goal: Walk in humility as Christ did. In your struggle with pride, you will actually see yourself as one who has:

1.   rights,

2.   equal or higher status than others, and

3.   special privileges because of what you have "earned."

Acts of humility can be the antidote for pride, if you do them for the Lord's glory and His Kingdom's benefit. When people treat you in a haughty manner, reach down deep inside yourself and say to yourself, "I am here to help them develop to their fullest potential so that God can receive the glory from their lives as well as from my life." Then proceed to be humble before them. Track how well you "walk" in humility over the next two weeks.

CHAPTER THIRTEEN

# ACHIEVING PRISTINE FOR THE MUNDANE

Read Chapter Thirteen in *Battle for the Mind*.

## THINGS TO PONDER

1.   When Jesus came to earth, "He gave up the expression, but He did not give up His godliness." What are some of the character traits that Jesus did not use while He was on earth? What are some of His character traits that we do see in His time on earth?

2.   Think about: *what Jesus wasn't*. Read Isaiah 53:2-3, and write down a list of those things that Jesus was not or did not receive. If you were like Jesus in all of these ways, receiving such rejection and being so despised, would you be able to love and sacrifice yourself, just as He did?

3.   Look at the list of things Jesus gave up. What have you given up or what will you give up in response to His example? Write something you will do beside each statement below.

- He gave up the pristine.

- He came and subjected Himself to nine months in a woman's womb as He wrapped Himself up in panoply of flesh. He held her up while she carried Him.

- He owned the cattle on a thousand hills, but was born in a manger.

- He subjected Himself to hunger even while He created all the food.

- He subjected Himself to exhaustion while He was the energy of the world.

- He subjected Himself to being questioned when He was above any question that anyone could ask.

- He subjected Himself to being ignored even though He has the power to cut off all oxygen.

- He was spat on and cursed. They mocked Him, but He kept the servant form.

- He subjected Himself to being ridiculed, dragged through three courts with a crown of thorns upon His head, flogged with a flagdrum, and hung on a cross. Still, He was God.

- He gave His life. He died on the Cross and was buried in a tomb. But He got up with *all power* because *He is Lord.*

## THINGS TO DO

Memorize Matthew 20:28: *"The Son of Man did not come to be served, but to serve, and to give His life a ransom for many."* Do you enter a room and see "being a servant" as your mission for your time with the people there? At the family table? In the boardroom at work? In the church committee meeting? Try speaking "service" to your spirit as you enter a room and see what happens.

## THINGS TO PRAY

In looking at the list of things that Jesus exposed Himself to for our sakes, think through how many of these you have had to endure. This can put your challenges and problems in a proper perspective. Though your cares are real, they need not consume you. Take time to lift your cares and challenges to the Lord, who has borne all of your trials before you were born. Allow the Holy Spirit to comfort you with His love. This isn't the false love that pats you on the shoulder and tells you everything will be all right. Let the true love of God envelop you. This love will hold you accountable for your part in the situation, but forgive you in an instant for anything you have done wrong. This love will embrace you, even when you have failed...again...and again.

CHAPTER FOURTEEN

# EXALTED TO THE HIGHEST PLACE

Read Chapter Fourteen in *Battle for the Mind*.

## THINGS TO PONDER

Lord Jesus' "power and authority encompasses every age and exceeds every known power, now and in the future."

- What does this mean to you?
- To what extent is His power and authority over your circumstances? Over people and relationships? Over authorities above you?

## THINGS TO RESEARCH

1. "The Lord Jesus Christ is the name that is above every name." Read what Chapter Fourteen has to say about the word *Lord*. Then look the word up in a standard dictionary and in a Bible dictionary.

- How is Christ Lord of all the earth?
- How is Christ Lord of your heart?

2. Using a concordance, look up the names of Jesus Christ and find where they are used in Scripture.

| OTHER NAMES USED FOR JESUS CHRIST | SCRIPTURE REFERENCES |
|---|---|
| Jehovah-Rohi, my shepherd | |
| Jehovah-Nissi, my banner | |
| Jehovah-MKaddesh, sanctifies me. | |
| Jehovah-Shalom, my peace | |
| Jehovah-Tsidkenu, my righteousness | |
| Jehovah-Rophe, my healer | |

| OTHER NAMES USED FOR JESUS CHRIST | SCRIPTURE REFERENCES |
|---|---|
| Jehovah-Jireh, my provider | |
| Jehovah-Sabaoth, the Lord of hosts | |

## THINGS TO DO

Memorize Philippians 2:11: *"That every tongue should confess that Jesus Christ is Lord, to the glory of God the Father."* When things seem out of control for you this week, confess this with your tongue. When you are caught off guard with yet another thing to do, confess this with your tongue. When you find yourself in the midst of a dilemma, confess this with your tongue. When someone misunderstands you, confess this with your tongue. When you make that same mistake again, confess this with your tongue. When something seems impossible, confess this with your tongue.

## THINGS TO PRAY

Jesus Christ is the answer to every need we have. Begin to praise Jesus for being Lord and Sovereign over all things and people, nations and worlds. Sing or pray these questions, followed by the answer—The Lord Jesus Christ!

- Who is this with power from on high?
- Who is this with healing in His hand?
- Who is this who can make day out of night?
- Who is this who can talk to a drug addict while he is high?
- Who is this who can take AIDS out of your blood?
- Who is this who can set you free from sin?

Now start adding your own questions, based on those situations and people who are on your heart. Shout His praise and make His name glorious!

CHAPTER FIFTEEN

# THEOLOGICAL AND PHILOSOPHICAL THOUGHTS AND CONCEPTS

Read the first section of Chapter Fifteen in *Battle for the Mind*

## THINGS TO PONDER

1. If you were to explain the theological view that the power of a humble mind is a mind of love, what would you say? What role does humility have in your relationship with God? What role does love play?

2. Do a summary of the philosophy section. Underline any outstanding words or phrases within the entries of each of the philosophers/theologians. How do the theological and philosophical viewpoints compare or contrast?

Read the second section of Chapter Fifteen—"Word Wealth."

## THINGS TO RESEARCH

1. Highlight anything that seems significant to you as you understand the nature of the words. Look up the following Scriptures that are quoted and read them in the context of the passage surrounding them.

- Philippians 2:6-7

- Philippians 2:9

2. Go through each of the "Use and Application" items at the end of each word entry. Why did the authors bring your attention to these? How does each of these principles set the standard for our thought processes and our actions?

Read the next section of Chapter Fifteen—"Practical Applications."

## THINGS TO REACH FOR (Goals)

Goal: Be able to apply your understanding of the theological and philosophical lessons learned in Chapters Eleven through Fourteen. Use this checklist to determine your progress. Circle each item as you evaluate where you are in the process.

Principle 1: "Adopt Christ's attitude of unselfishness, servanthood, humility, and obedience."

- I understand this principle intellectually.
- I believe this principle and am ready to exercise the faith to operate in it.
- I am operating in the understanding of this principle.
- I am able to disciple someone else to walk in this principle.

Principle 2: "Adopt attitudinal characteristics for maintaining unity and living unselfishly."

- I understand this principle intellectually.
- I believe this principle and am ready to exercise the faith to operate in it.
- I am operating in the understanding of this principle.
- I am able to disciple someone else to walk in this principle.

Principle 3: "Seek to be one in spirit with other members. The Church ought to be one in spirit because the Spirit of Christ unites the Church into one body."

- I understand this principle intellectually.
- I believe this principle and am ready to exercise the faith to operate in it.
- I am operating in the understanding of this principle.
- I am able to disciple someone else to walk in this principle.

Principle 4: "Understand the basis and importance of unity."

- I understand this principle intellectually.
- I believe this principle and am ready to exercise the faith to operate in it.

- I am operating in the understanding of this principle.

- I am able to disciple someone else to walk in this principle.

Principle 5: "Regard, consider, count, and esteem others as more important than self."

- I understand this principle intellectually.

- I believe this principle and am ready to exercise the faith to operate in it.

- I am operating in the understanding of this principle.

- I am able to disciple someone else to walk in this principle.

Principle 6: "Understand that giving up self for service to others is truly the power of a humble mind because humility with love brings honor and exaltation."

- I understand this principle intellectually.

- I believe this principle and am ready to exercise the faith to operate in it.

- I am operating in the understanding of this principle.

- I am able to disciple someone else to walk in this principle.

The next section of Chapter Fifteen—"Action Steps"—follows in an expanded form.

## THINGS TO DO

Review the Memory Verses from Section Three. Memorization should help you utilize these verses in the days and weeks to come.

- Romans 15:5-6

- John 8:32

- Philippians 2:5

- Matthew 20:28

- Philippians 2:11

## THINGS TO PRAY AND LEARN

1.   "The first step is to prayerfully read and meditate on Philippians 2:1-11. As Christ Jesus willingly laid aside His heavenly glory to come to earth and die, we should be willing to adopt Christ's attitude of unselfishness, servanthood, humility, and obedience, and look beyond our own interest for the sake of others." Though we have read these words often during this section, meditate on them to let the Holy Spirit speak to you as to how you can show forth His glory to an increasingly greater capacity as you humble yourself.

2.   "Think about what it means to have the mind-set of Christ. You must show evidence of selflessness and humility while considering the needs of others as your top priority." Rate yourself on how you currently conduct yourself in the following mind-sets, on a scale of 1 to 10, with 10 being the highest. Then condense the statement down to four words or less so that you can remember it easier and remind yourself of the Christ-like attitude you are seeking.

|  | 1 | 2 | 3 | 4 | 5 | 6 | 7 | 8 | 9 | 10 |
|---|---|---|---|---|---|---|---|---|---|---|
| Evidence of Christ-like attitude |  |  |  |  |  |  |  |  |  |  |
| Encourage and motivate others in your daily living." |  |  |  |  |  |  |  |  |  |  |
| "Witness to others in your daily living." |  |  |  |  |  |  |  |  |  |  |
| Avoid doing things with self-serving motives |  |  |  |  |  |  |  |  |  |  |

|  | 1 | 2 | 3 | 4 | 5 | 6 | 7 | 8 | 9 | 10 |
|---|---|---|---|---|---|---|---|---|---|---|
| "'In lowliness of mind esteem others as being better than self.' | | | | | | | | | | |
| Look out not only for own interests, but also for the interests of others | | | | | | | | | | |
| Avoid self-centeredness and a spirit of selfishness | | | | | | | | | | |

3.   "Conduct your life so that others may see you as a Gospel sermon— *Let this mind be in you which was also in Christ Jesus.*" Paul told Timothy that he should let people see his process of maturing so they could watch him grow and desire the same. Think about specific ways that you could implement the following mind-sets in your life, signifying a change for the better and being a witness of God's grace maturing you. Jot down ideas beside each one.

- "Be humble, and in humility think more of each other than you do of yourselves. Never act from motives of rivalry or personal vanity."

- "Cultivate a spirit of authentic Christian humility that would be evidenced by a willingness to regard others as more important than self."

- "Show and express love toward other believers and non-believers—relatives, friends, neighbors, and coworkers. You are to humble yourself and treat them with love and dignity because it is the right thing to do."

- "Be humble, thinking of others as better than yourself. Don't be selfish; don't live to make a good impression on others."

- "Give up self for service to others—truly the power of a humble mind."

4.  Read John 3:16 and reread Philippians 2:4-8 to understand that the sacrifice of Christ is both the proof of His love and the standard of our own love for others." Using the verses above, write down the phrases from Philippians 2:4-8 that correspond with the phrases in John 3:16.

| JOHN 3:16 | PHILIPPIANS 2:4-8 |
|---|---|
| *For God so loved the world* | |
| *That He gave His one and only Son* | |
| *That whoever believes on Him* | |
| *Shall not perish* | |
| *But have eternal life.* | |

"Then ask yourself, 'Am I willing to humble myself, even sacrifice myself, in the best interest of another?'" Pray through the two attitudes below, asking the Holy Spirit to strengthen you to be able to do these easily.

- "Always ask yourself, 'What would Jesus do?'"

- "Imagine Jesus doing the things that you are doing or thinking the things that you are thinking; then reflect on how you would compare Jesus' attitude and action to your attitude and action."

5.   "Read John 13:3-17 to understand that Jesus' act of washing the disciples' feet demonstrated love. Jesus was their teacher and Lord, meaning He was on a higher level than the disciples, yet He assumed a position of humility and service because He loved those He served."

- What are practical ways that you can practice humility, servanthood, and love?

- Look at the suggestions below and write a specific idea you have for each one, naming the person, group, or situation that you will serve. Be sure the way in which you perform each act lifts up Jesus and not you.

- Pray that pride would not enter into your acts of humility.

- "Practice being humble by serving others and committing yourself to doing things that you think are beneath you. Remember, you cannot have unity without humility, and you will not humble yourself to anybody you don't love."

- "Perform a menial task to teach a lesson in humility and self-less service because, ultimately, servanthood is a disposition of the heart and spirit, which expresses itself in concrete action."

6. "Ask for wisdom to know the secret things of God. His Spirit will reveal them to you, for you have the mind of Christ because the Spirit of Christ lives in you." Be sure to leave yourself enough time to not only make this request known to the Lord, but also to listen to the Spirit's response. Look at Solomon's prayer of wisdom in 1 Kings 3:6-9 and read it aloud to the Lord as a prayer.

7. "Read and meditate on John 17:22. It is critical to understand that Christ Jesus also prayed for the future believers that they might be one." Think of the ways in which the Father and the Son are one. Are we able to experience the same oneness with other believers?

8. "Recognize that it is what you put into practice from God's Word that brings blessing to yourself and others." Every time you enter God's Word this week, be sure to take one thing out to put into practice. That means that when you hear Sunday's sermon, you must do one thing that reflects the message. Each day as you read the Word, you must take one thing and apply it to that day's activities. Allow the Word to enrich your intellect and then enrich your service.

## THINGS TO REVIEW

Reread the chapter titles and section titles in Chapters Eleven through Fourteen. What summary statements can you give about what you have learned from this Section?

PART FOUR

# FINDING PEACE THROUGH PRAISE

Read the Introduction to Part Four in *Battle for the Mind*.

## THINGS TO PONDER

1. "Contrary to what people think, peace is not mind over matter. You cannot talk your way into peace." What does this mean to you?

- How do you get peace?
- What does peace have to do with the focus of your mind?

2. When "you begin to see yourself and your world through the eyes of God, you will tap into tranquility and true happiness." How is it possible to see yourself through God's eyes? When you look at the world from God's perspective, what changes in your line of vision?

## THINGS TO DO

We tend to think of peace as something that is exchanged horizontally between people or nations on earth. But it is the peace of God that brings true earthly peace. Have you seen "false peace" where it seemed like there was peace, but tension was building underneath so much that the peace ended in an explosion? How does true peace prohibit tensions from undermining it? Write *think vertical* on a card and put it on your desk for this week. As you go throughout your tasks at your desk, let these words remind you of where you can obtain true peace.

## THINGS TO PRAY

Praise your way into peace. Take an extended praise time. Use songs, psalms, Scripture, hymns, and spiritual songs to align your spirit with the Holy Spirit and bask in His peace. Lift up a challenge or problem you are currently facing and continue to praise God until you feel peace, even when you think about that challenge.

# THINGS TO REACH FOR (Goals)

My Goal: To obtain true peace—"peace like a river will flood your soul." "Once your thoughts have been transformed so you focus vertically rather than horizontally, then peace like a river will flood your soul."

CHAPTER SIXTEEN

# REJOICE ALWAYS

Read Chapter Sixteen in *Battle for the Mind*.

## THINGS TO PONDER

1.   "...Paul, though a prisoner, was exultantly happy and calls us to be full of joy and to rejoice always." Would you describe yourself as someone who is "exultantly happy"?

- What is the difference between someone who appears to be happy (some almost giddy) and someone who truly is?

- How do we become like the apostle Paul?

- What connection did he make between the power of his mind and his ability to rejoice?

2.   "To rejoice is the central core of why we were created." What does this mean to you?

- How are "giving God glory" and "rejoicing before Him" connected? How is true joy found only in the Lord?

- Why is joy a fruit of the Spirit?

3.   Philippians 4:13 says, *"I can do all things through Christ who strengthens me."* Is this easy for you to believe intellectually?

- Is this easy for you to put into practice?

- Where have you found this principle true in your life?

- Where have you watched God strengthen you beyond your own ability?

- Where has this been difficult to believe? Remember, either this statement is totally true or totally false because it does not give us the words *few* or *some*, but the word *all*.

4. "Our inner attitudes do not have to reflect our outward circumstances." Think through what this means to you.

Why and how do some people wear masks and hide their inner feelings?

- Is this what this statement means?

- What is the cause and effect of what is going on outside of you and what is going on inside of you?

5. "Rejoicing is to be a constant discipline." It is not intermittent, not occasional, not just a good intention. How is this steady stream of rejoicing possible to a normal human being going through life's cache of problems and challenges?

## THINGS TO RESEARCH

1. Using a concordance, look up the following words that are used in Paul's letters to the Romans, the Corinthians, the Ephesians, the Colossians, the Philippians, and the Thessalonians. Look up the verses and read them in context. Write down anything that the Holy Spirit teaches you during your study.

- Rejoice/ rejoicing

- Joy

2. Read Nehemiah 8:10 in your Bible. Reread it in the context. Ask several people to give you a story of when they found this to be true for them. Think through what they learned and compare it with your experience.

- How do you gain strength from joy that comes from the Lord?

3. Read Habakkuk 3:17-18 in your Bible. Reread it in the context of the chapter. Highlight anything that speaks to your heart.

- No matter how grave the situation is, rejoicing is your only choice. Why?

## THINGS TO DO

1. Memorize Philippians 4:4: *"Rejoice in the Lord always. Again I will say, rejoice!"* Is this a request or a command?

- Does it have exceptions attached to it?

- Is it bound by circumstances, events, seasons, or times?

- Is it dependent upon relationships or feelings?

- Use this verse as a carte blanche summons to obedience. *Rejoice!*

2. "True faith never says, 'I cannot.' We have the freedom to rejoice always."

- Write *I can!!!* On a card and put it by your bedside table. Every day as you awake, read this and declare it by faith. Make your day a positive experience, not because you have self-talked your way into it, but because God has awakened the mustard seed of faith inside of you. What does this mean?

## THINGS TO PRAY

1. "Since you are connected to God thought His Spirit, you can rejoice as you look through the eyes of faith to see that God has planned for you to praise, to worship, and to thank Him for His faithfulness, no matter how devastating the circumstances." List several things that need your attention in prayer. Pray for each one, but avoid stating the situation. Instead, focus on praising God for what is needed in the situation. If you need to see God's provision, for example, praise Him as your provider. Remind Him of the provision that He gave to the Israelites in the wilderness and to Elijah in the desert. Remind and thank Him for the provision that He has given you thus far. Let your praise claim "that God is above the situation." Worship Him as you commune with your personal provider.

2. Dedicate one of your prayer times this week to making statements of faith. (See the ones that are given as examples in Chapter Sixteen—Rejoice Always.) Praise God for the process He is taking you through. Praise and rejoice for every aspect of any challenge that gives you hope. Look at the good and even the possible good that awaits the conclusion of the matter.

## THINGS TO REACH FOR (Goals)

Goal: Rejoicing becomes a lifelong occupation. This is possible because "the Spirit of Christ, the Living Water, is constantly flowing through your transformed and renewed mind." When you decide on a career, you study to become skilled for the job you will have. You put in the hours necessary to complete your assigned tasks. When you want to move up the business ladder, you make excellence your standard. It is, therefore, imperative that you make joy your lifelong occupation. Study it over a long period of time to understand how and when to rejoice. Put the hours into prayer in order to change negative mind-sets that deliver negative behaviors. Become an excellent "rejoicer," making joy your standard.

CHAPTER SEVENTEEN

# YOU ARE WHAT YOU THINK

Read Chapter Seventeen in *Battle for the Mind*.

## THINGS TO PONDER

1.  "It is what you think about yourself that gives significance to who you are. What you think about yourself can elevate or decline your position." Since your thinking process is an "equation," write a mathematical equation or sentence symbolizing how you think about yourself.

- Do you think you are greater than you really are? Why or why not?

- Do you think less of yourself than you should? Why or why not?

- Does your self-knowledge increase or decrease your overall knowledge?

2.  The authors tell us that the "mind is a place of evaluation, and in order to evaluate, you must be objective about subjective things."

- What does this statement say to you?

- How can you "stay free" from "the contamination" that comes to your mind?

3.  "Your mind is too powerful for you to allow it to turn against you."

- What does this statement mean to you?

- How do you fight the environmental battles that surround you?

- How do you stave off evil spirits?

- How do you become a conduit for the power of God?

- How do you offset the negativity of your environment with the creativity of the Spirit?

## THINGS TO RESEARCH

1. Ask some Christians that you know the following questions:

- "Can someone be thinking of praising God, while at the same time, not thinking of joy and rejoicing?"

- Ask them to explain their answer and to give an example from their own lives.

From your survey, can you conclude that "the mind is attached to the source, which is the power of God, while at the same time, the mind is also connected to the flesh—the body—and the body is connected to your environment, issues, and circumstances"?

2. "Your mind is rooted in biblical precept." Look up the following passages and write down what they say about how believers are to conduct themselves:

| SCRIPTURAL REFERENCE | HOW BELIEVERS ARE TO CONDUCT THEMSELVES ACCORDING TO THIS SCRIPTURE |
|---|---|
| Matthew 22:37 | |
| Mark 12:30 | |
| Luke 10:27 | |
| Acts 4:32 | |
| 1 Corinthians 1:10 | |
| 2 Corinthians 13:11 | |
| 1 Corinthians 14:15 | |

## THINGS TO DO

1. Go back to the Chapter Five "Word Wealth" section and review the entry for the word *mind*.

- What is contained within the concept of the mind to indicate the whole person?

- How does the mind go beyond intellect?

- Where do the concepts of the mind and the spirit intersect?

- How does your mind deal with your consciousness?

2.   Memorize Philippians 4:6: *"Be anxious for nothing, but in everything, by prayer and supplication, with thanksgiving, let your requests be made known to God."* The words nothing and everything are absolute; there are no exceptions! How well do you follow the prescription this verse holds?

## THINGS TO PRAY

1.   How do you "reject negative thoughts from your mind?" Take time to lift any negative circumstances in your life to the Lord right now. Then begin your process of rejecting them. Speak the promises of God about those circumstances. Begin to warm your heart with the Spirit of God and praise Him for His nature that is sovereign over your circumstances.

2.   "Praise releases us, but negative condemnation, including negative thoughts and criticism, restricts and controls us." Our spiritual minds must maintain control over negative thoughts. Take an extended time of praise each day this week, proclaiming God's greatness and giving Him thanks for the good things He has done for you. Fill your mind with Him to secure your mind for the day.

## THINGS TO REACH FOR (GOALS)

Goal: Release negative thoughts. "When you release the negative thoughts, the Spirit of Christ guards you with His peace." Using your prayer activity above, set a goal to discontinue negative thinking. Place a marker in your day planner or calendar at each day for the next weeks that says "release and peace." After the two week period, check your progress.

CHAPTER EIGHTEEN

# DON'T WORRY, BE HAPPY

Read Chapter Eighteen in *Battle for the Mind*.

## THINGS TO PONDER

1.  The authors maintain that when "you worry, you are saying that you don't trust that God will provide for your needs."

    - How is worry connected to trust?

    - How many of your worries are due to vain imaginations (things that will never happen or situations that are of very little significance)?

    - How can you replace worry with trust?

    - How can prayer replace worry in your mind?

    - In what way is praise an antidote to worry?

    - Describe how praise works as catharsis.

    - How has praise done this work in your life thus far?

2.  "Faith is based on knowledge of God's Word and His character."

    - How does God's Word influence your faith?

    - How does knowledge of God's character influence your faith?

    - Why does the world lose its controlling influence over your mind when you stand in faith?

3.  Think about several different words for prayer. How do you use these in your own prayer life?

    - *Prayer*—general term for communication with God

    - *Supplication/petition*—requests for particular benefits

    - *Thanksgiving*—grateful acknowledgement of past mercies

▪ *Requests*—individual desires that form part of the whole prayer

## THINGS TO RESEARCH

1.  Use your concordance and look up the words *worry, anxious,* and *anxiety.* Find Scriptures that use these words and see what you can find out about:

- why worry occurs,

- how to handle worry, and

- how some people worried while others trusted God.

2.  "The Hebrew word for faith (*emeth*) connotes faithfulness, which equals trusted, trustworthy, or confidence and trust in God and in God's Word." Look up the following words in a standard dictionary and a Bible dictionary. Note anything that helps you understand these better.

- *Faith*

- Trust

- Confidence

3.  "The writer of Hebrews provides a description of how *faith* works, instead of a definition of *faith.*"

- How does faith work in your life? Look up the Hebrews' Hall of Faith in chapter 11.

- As you read about the different people the writer mentions, note how faith worked for each person.

- What did they have faith for? What was the result of their exercise of faith?

## THINGS TO DO

1.  Memorize Philippians 4:8: *"Finally, brethren, whatever things are true, whatever things are noble, whatever things are just, whatever things are pure, whatever things are lovely, whatever things are of good report, if there is any virtue and if there is anything praiseworthy—meditate on these things."*

List ten things that you know are true, noble, just, pure, lovely, of good report, virtuous, and praiseworthy:

| 10 Things That Are True | 10 Things That Are Noble | 10 Things That Are Just | 10 Things That Are Pure | 10 Things That Are Lovely | 10 Things That Are Of Good Report | 10 Things That Are Virtuous | 10 Things That Are Praise-worthy |
|---|---|---|---|---|---|---|---|
| | | | | | | | |
| | | | | | | | |
| | | | | | | | |
| | | | | | | | |
| | | | | | | | |
| | | | | | | | |
| | | | | | | | |
| | | | | | | | |
| | | | | | | | |
| | | | | | | | |

Now, looking at your list, you have 80 things that are more profitable to think about than problems or negative situations. Read these aloud and declare them to your mind.

2.  Take a newspaper and prove this statement: "The spirit of the world is in opposition to God." Find articles, opinions, and editorials that show the spirit of the world. Pray for each item that God's Kingdom would come and His will would be done.

3.  "Don't worry; pray. The word for 'prayer'...means prayer as worship." Make yourself a nice sign that says, "Don't worry; pray." Stick it in an obvious place. See what reactions it gets from other people. Set your will to replace worry with prayer.

## THINGS TO PRAY

1.   "Faith is the title deed of things hoped for...assurance rests on God's promises...it is only by faith that we come to know the love of Christ Jesus... faith is not something that we produce; it is what God's Word produces in us." Go through the four steps given here in your prayer time. First, speak out loud those things that you are currently hoping for. Next, speak what God's promises are about each thing you are hoping for. Next, allow the love of Christ to infiltrate your list of God's promises and your requests. Finally, speak the pure Word of God about each request.

2.   Pray Matthew 6:25-27,34, inserting your name and meditating on the principles and directives that Jesus gives.

> *Therefore I say to you [name], [name] do not worry about your life, what you will eat or what you will drink, not about your body, what you will put on.... [name], look at the birds of the air, for they neither sow nor reap nor gather into barns; yet your heavenly Father feeds them. Are you [name] not of more value then they? [Can you, name], by worrying, add one cubit to your stature? ...Therefore, [name] do not worry about tomorrow, for tomorrow will worry about its own thing. Sufficient for the day is its own trouble.*

Now raise your hands in worship, releasing anything that causes you to worry.

## THINGS TO REACH FOR (Goals)

Goal: Choose to be content in all circumstances. Many of us are afraid to ask God to give us patience because we believe we will be deluged with attacks to test the patience we seek. But you need not fear—when the Holy Spirit instructs you, you are truly able to rise above whatever the attack or purifying fire delivers. In the same way, you need to come to God boldly and ask Him to make you content in all circumstances. Though you must "continue to pray in faith for what you need and praise God for all He has done," you are to be ready for those things that may test whether your contentment is truly born of God or of yourself. Make the goal to choose contentment as a spiritual point of growth. Pray each day this month to seek God's perspective on where you need to grow in satisfaction. Track your progress each week as you continue in His school of contentment.

CHAPTER NINETEEN

# PRAISE BRINGS PEACE THAT TRANSCENDS UNDERSTANDING

Read Chapter Nineteen in *Battle for the Mind*.

## THINGS TO PONDER

1.  The authors say that "true peace comes from knowing that God is in control and not just from positive thinking." To put this principle into operation, you first must intellectually embrace its truth. Then you must know how to receive blessings from God. Finally, you need to be in a receiving "position" in order to catch the peace as He hands it to you.

2.  "You are in spiritual combat, guarded and protected by God's power and peace as your sentinels or patrols, surrounding the perimeter of your mind." Close your eyes and begin to picture this. What is a weak spot in your mind? Imagine a fully trained, armed patrol guarding that weak area so that nothing can penetrate it. What kind of comfort does this picture give to you? This isn't just vain imagination, is it? How does God send peace like a soldier to protect you from destructive thoughts?

3.  You may not "feel absolutely at ease and relived after you pray." Why not? When you pray for peace, what do you receive? What are the indicators that God is doing something with and for you?

4.  "When you rejoice and praise God, He guards your mind with His peace." How are praise and rejoicing connected to peace? Do you know anyone who keeps praising God in the midst of a trying circumstance, but it seems like that person is just trying to talk himself or herself into feeling better, and it truly does not seem real? How does true praise make you less of a religious fanatic and bring your closer to the Spirit of God?

## THINGS TO RESEARCH

1.  Ask some Christian friends to give you their explanation of Psalm 86:12—*"I will praise You, O Lord my God, with all my heart...,"* and Psalm

34:1—*"I will extol the Lord at all times; His praise will always be on my lips"* (NIV). There are two all's and an always in these verses.

- Is this behavior possible? Why or why not?

- From your research, consider how praise and rejoicing transforms you by renewing your mind.

- How does worship help you identify God for who He is and what He does?

## THINGS TO DO

1. "Prayer and peace are closely connected. When you pray, you can push back the attack of your circumstances and your situation, defeat the tormenting thoughts in your mind, and claim the victory in order to experience peace of mind." Write this equation on a card:

PRAYER = (PUSH BACK ATTACK) + (DEFEAT ENEMY)
+ (CLAIM VICTORY) = PEACE.

Put this in your wallet, where you will see it every time you open it. Then think about whether you need to *stop* right then and pray to get peace.

2. Memorize Philippians 4:7: *"And the peace of God, which surpasses all understanding, will guard your hearts and minds through Christ Jesus."* Though the challenges you face may be large, and logically, you do not see any way out, the peace of God is larger and is beyond all logic. So, the next time you have a challenge, shake your head and laugh. The peace of God is greater than anything that can try to shake you.

## THINGS TO PRAY

1. God's peace surrounds your heart, mind, emotions, appetite, soul, and spirit. Take time to ask the Holy Spirit to show you true peace. This may take some time. If you are not currently facing a challenge, you may not have anything specific to apply the peace of God toward. However, you still need peace so that when trouble comes knocking, you will be strong enough to slam the door of peace in its face. If you do have a specific challenge facing you, take time to apply peace to that

problem and rid your mind of the harmful outside forces that want to attack you.

2.   Pray the following Scriptures, meditating on the words and amplifying the concepts as you grow in faith and peace.

> *Giving thanks always for all things to God the Father in the name of our Lord Jesus Christ* (Ephesians 5:20).

> *In everything give thanks: for this is the will of God in Christ Jesus for you* (1 Thessalonians 5:18).

> *Be anxious for nothing, but in everything by prayer and supplication, with thanksgiving, let your requests be made known to God; and the peace of God, which passes all understanding, will guard your hearts and minds through Christ Jesus* (Philippians 4:6-7).

"Your future will be better than your past because peace in the heart will follow praying about your concern."

3.   The authors give the following liberating statements that can bring a truer reality to your mind than the one you have when you are darkened through a worldly mind-set. Take time in prayer to speak these things audibly. Speak them with conviction and allow the Holy Spirit to make them real to your spirit.

- I have the desire and the will to be creative, victorious, and the best I can be.
- I must not allow my thoughts to overpower my will.
- I will not allow others to control my will by controlling my mind or my thoughts.
- I can do all things because the Spirit of Christ has renewed my mind.
- I can now change my circumstances.
- I am a child of God. The Lord Jesus is my Savior, and I belong to Him.
- I am in Christ and not under condemnation.

- I am healed, delivered, and set free.

- I am transformed, and I have a renewed mind.

- I am beautiful, extraordinary, magnanimous, and very special to God.

- I am blessed and anointed.

- I am rejoicing and praising God at all times.

- I have the mind of Christ, and the Spirit of Christ dwells in me.

- I can win all mind games through Christ who strengthens me.

- Rejoice, and again I say, rejoice.

## THINGS TO REACH FOR (Goals)

1.   Goal: "Never keep a trouble half an hour on your own mind before you tell it to God." Spurgeon gave us the goal for this chapter. He also said that "the longer you take telling your trouble to God, the more your peace will be impaired." Keep Isaiah 26:3 before you, *"Thou wilt keep him in perfect peace, whose mind is stayed on Thee; because he trusteth in Thee"* (KJV). As soon as a trouble comes your way, take note of the time. Literally, find a way to take the trouble to God in prayer within 30 minutes of the onset of the challenge. Perhaps you will have to go to the restroom at the office to pray. Perhaps you will need to put the kids down for a "quiet time" while you pray. But begin this regimen and see what changes take place in your mental outlook about the specific trouble and about problems in general.

2.   Goal: Give up self for service to others. As you rejoice, you have the mind of Christ. When you have the mind of Christ, you can partake of the same prophesy that was spoken about Him. Speak this Scripture out loud and proclaim it.

> *The Spirit of the Lord God is upon me, because the Lord has anointed me to preach good tidings to the poor; He has sent me to heal the brokenhearted, to proclaim liberty to the captives, and the opening of the prison to those who are bound; to proclaim the acceptable year of the Lord...* (Isaiah 61:1-2).

Consider each day this week as a "mission." Become God's missionary wherever you go, and look for opportunities to bring these elements of Christ to others.

CHAPTER TWENTY

# THEOLOGICAL AND PHILOSOPHICAL THOUGHTS AND CONCEPTS

Read the first section of Chapter Twenty in *Battle for the Mind*.

## THINGS TO PONDER

1.   If you were to explain the theological understanding of joy in the life of a Christian, what would you say? From what you understand about rejoicing, do you see how it can change people's minds despite the circumstances they find themselves facing?

2.   Explain or summarize the theological and/or philosophical thoughts and concepts presented in Chapter Twenty. Underline any outstanding words or phrases within the entries of each of the philosophers/theologians. How do the theological and philosophical viewpoints compare or contrast?

Read the second section of Chapter Twenty—"Word Wealth."

## THINGS TO RESEARCH

1.   Highlight anything that seems significant to you as you understand the nature of the words. Look up the following Scriptures and read them in the context of the passage surrounding them.

- Philippians 4:4

- Luke 10:20

- Romans 12:12

- Romans 15:13

- Galatians 5:22

- Philippians 2:17-18

- Colossians 1:11-12

- Colossians 1:24

2.  Go through each of the "Use and Application" items at the end of each word entry. Why did the authors bring your attention to these? How do these principles set the standard for your thought processes and your actions?

Read the next section of Chapter Twenty—"Practical Applications."

## THINGS TO REACH FOR (Goals)

Goal: Be able to apply your understanding of the theological and philosophical lessons learned in Chapters Sixteen through Nineteen. Use this checklist to determine your progress. Circle each item as you evaluate where you are in the process.

Principle 1: "You must refuse to worry about things because Christ Jesus gives peace to those who trust Him and ask for His help."

- I understand this principle intellectually.
- I believe this principle and am ready to exercise the faith to operate in it.
- I am operating in the understanding of this principle.
- I am able to disciple someone else to walk in this principle.

Principle 2: "Rejoice and be contented in all circumstances. This joy is to be experienced always."

- I understand this principle intellectually.
- I believe this principle and am ready to exercise the faith to operate in it.
- I am operating in the understanding of this principle.
- I am able to disciple someone else to walk in this principle.

Principle 3: "Understand that rejoicing is a constant discipline."

- I understand this principle intellectually.
- I believe this principle and am ready to exercise the faith to operate in it.

- I am operating in the understanding of this principle.

- I am able to disciple someone else to walk in this principle.

Principle 4: "Understand that you rejoice because true joy is in the Lord."

- I understand this principle intellectually.

- I believe this principle and am ready to exercise the faith to operate in it.

- I am operating in the understanding of this principle.

- I am able to disciple someone else to walk in this principle.

The next section of Chapter Twenty—"Action Steps"—follows in an expanded form.

## THINGS TO DO

Review the Memory Verses from Section Four. Memorization should help you utilize these verses in the days and weeks to come.

| SCRIPTURAL REFERENCE | HOW I WILL UTILIZE THIS BIBLICAL CONCEPT |
|---|---|
| Philippians 4:4 | |
| Philippians 4:6 | |
| Philippians 4:7 | |
| Philippians 4:8 | |

## THINGS TO PRAY AND LEARN

1. "Prayerfully and carefully reread the Book of Philippians...This book is truly a masterpiece full of tenderness, warmth, affection, joy, and rejoicing." Take a section and pray it. Sometimes you might pray it out loud and declare what it says. For some sections, you may need to prostrate yourself and be humbled under the mighty hand of God. There are sections that should help you connect with the love that the Father has for you.

2.   Memorize Philippians 4:4-7. You have already learned verses 4, 6, 7, and 8. Just learn verse 5 to make the passage complete. "Allow the truth of the text to order your thinking and your life. The ultimate purpose is for you to love God with your mind and to trust Him at all times." This is a good passage to pray on the way to work or another regular activity.

3.   "Rejoice in spite of trials." Read this section in the book. Below, write a Scripture reference that supports each statement:

| BIBLICAL STATEMENT | SCRIPTURE REFERENCE |
| --- | --- |
| Pray and thank the Lord for taking you through this situation. | |
| Praise God for who He is and what He has already done for you. | |
| *Praise the Lord, for the Lord is good; sing praises and _____ to His name, for it is pleasant.* | Ps. 135:3 |
| *Sing aloud to God our strength; make a joyful _____ to God.* | Ps. 81:1 |
| Confess your sin because, *"If we confess our sins, He is faithful and just to forgive us our sins and to cleanse us from all unrighteousness"* (1 John 1:9). | |
| Pray as though everything depends on God; at the same time, you are to do all that you can to change the situation. | |
| Rejoice in the joy of others. Rejoice when others are blessed and honored. | |
| *Let your gentleness be known to all people. The Lord is at hand* (Phil 4:5). Everyone who comes into contact with you should experience gentleness, moderation, and patience. | |
| Show respect for family members and close friends, not just the people you're trying to influence spiritually. | |

| BIBLICAL STATEMENT | SCRIPTURE REFERENCE |
|---|---|
| Be gentle and kind to everyone and practice saying nice things to friends, family, and strangers. | |
| Give a word of encouragement and show appreciation for the little things. Be responsible and let other people know that they can depend upon you. | |

4.    Here are some "reasons to rejoice and offer praise." Look at the statements below. Pray through each reason until your spirit resounds with the Holy Spirit.

- Rejoice because God commands you to rejoice always.

- Rejoice because Christ Jesus loves you and He died for your salvation.

- Remember, God's written Word is always relevant, powerful, and alive. The Word says, *"Rejoice in the Lord always. Again I will say, rejoice"* (Phil. 4:4). Don't forget the word *always*.

- Believe that God loves you and that He will never leave you. Knowing that God loves you and that He wants to communicate with your spirit gives you the strength to carry on—no matter what difficulties you are facing. Just knowing that *"the joy of the Lord is your strength"* (Neh. 8:10) will bring peace and comfort at all times and in all circumstances.

- When you encounter a situation that is stressful or difficult and you don't feel happy, you can still be joyful on the inside as you rejoice and delight in the Lord.

## THINGS TO REVIEW

1.    Reread the chapter titles and section titles in chapters Sixteen through Nineteen. What summary statements can you give about what you have learned from this section?

2. Review all the memory verses from the entire study. Make a point to review these each month.

3. Review all the goals that you made during this study. Check your progress and write reminders for any that are still in process.

# ENDNOTES

## SECTION ONE INTRODUCTION

1. Saint Augustine, *The Confessions of Saint Augustine* (A.D. 401), translated by Edward Bouverie Pusey; http://www.sacred-texts.com/chr/augconf.htm; accessed February 1, 2012.

2. Martin Luther, *Works*, Weimar edition, Vol. 54, 179ff; cited in Bruce, 59; cited on *Bible.org;* http://www.bible.org/page.asp?page_id=2285#P127_9841; accessed January 18, 2012.

3. Howard Snyder, *The Radical Wesley* (Downers Grove, IL: IVP, 1980), 26.

4. Martin Luther, Andrew Thornton, translator, *Martin Luther's Preface to the Epistle to the Romans in Present Truth,* Volume 12, Article 6, Part 2.

5. *Ibid.*

## PART ONE INTRODUCTION

1. G.K. Chesterton, *Orthodoxy* (Colorado Springs, CO: Harold Shaw Publishers, 1994), 24.

## CHAPTER ONE

1. *Blue Letter Bible,* Romans 8:1, s.v. "Katakrima" (Strong's Greek 2631); http://www.blueletterbible.org/lang/lexicon/lexicon.cfm?Strongs=G2631&t=KJV; accessed February 1, 2012.

2. *Blue Letter Bible*, s.v. "Nephesh" (Strong's Hebrew 5315); http://www.blueletterbible.org/lang/lexicon/Lexicon.cfm?strongs=H5315; accessed February 1, 2012.

3. Dan J. Love, *The Mind of Yahweh, Basic Understanding Series* (July 22, 2003); http:www.sabbbatarian.com/TableContent/MindodYHWH.html; accessed March 18, 2005.

4. Michael Czapokay Sudduth, "The Prospects for 'Mediate' Natural Theology in John Calvin," *Religious Studies* (March 1995); http://philofreligion.homestead.com/files/calvinpaper.htm; accessed January 18, 2012.

5. Aristotle, *On The Soul*, cited in "Aristotle," *Internet Encyclopedia of Philosophy*; http://www.iep.utm.edu/aristotl/; accessed January 18, 2012.

6. *Ibid.*

7. *Blue Letter Bible*, s.v. "Phroneo" (Strong's Greek 5426); http://www .blueletterbible.org/lang/lexicon/Lexicon.cfm?strongs=G5426; accessed February 1, 2012.

## CHAPTER TWO

1. René Descartes, *Discourse on Method* (New York: Barnes and Noble Publishing, Inc., 2004), 82.

2. *Ibid.*, 130.

3. Peter Hanns Refil and Ellen Judy Wilson, *Encyclopedia of the Enlightenment* (New York: Book Builders Inc., 1996), 206.

4. Michael Czapokay Sudduth, "The Prospects for 'Mediate' Natural Theology in John Calvin," *Religious Studies* (March 1995); http://philofreligion.homestead .com/files/calvinpaper.htm; accessed January 18, 2012.

5. C.A. Anderson Scott, *Christianity According to St. Paul* (London, N.W: Cambridge University Press, 1961), 99.

## CHAPTER THREE

1. *Bible Study Tools,* s.v. "Peh" (Strong's Hebrew 6310); http://www.biblestudytools .com/lexicons/hebrew/nas/peh.html; accessed February 1, 2012.

2. John Herrin, "Yahweh, His Breath and His Word" *Heart 4 God* (18 June 2003); http://www.heart4god.ws/HTMLobj-1963/Yahweh__His_Breath_and_His _Word.pdf; accessed February 1, 2012.

3. René Descartes, *Discourse on Method* (New York: Barnes and Noble Publishing, Inc., 2004), 108.

4. *Blue Letter Bible,* s.v. "Leb" (Strong's Hebrew 3820); http://www.blueletterbible .org/lang/lexicon/Lexicon.cfm?strongs=H3820; accessed February 1, 2012.

5. Blaise Pascal, *Pensees* (London, England: Penguin Group, translated 1995), 28.

6. "Holman Bible Dictionary: Wind," *Study Light*; http://www.studylight.org/dic/ hbd/view.cgi?number=T6458; accessed February 1, 2012.

## CHAPTER FIVE

1. René Descartes, *Discourse on Method*, 130.

2. J.P. Moreland and William Lane Craig, *Philosophical Foundations for a Christian Worldview* (Madison, WI: InterVasity Press, 2003), 507.

3. René Descartes, *Discourse on Method* (New York: Barnes and Noble Publishing, Inc., 2004), 130.

4. *Ibid.*

5. Marian Hillar, "Philo of Alexandria," *Internet Encyclopedia of Philosophy;* http://www.iep.utm.edu/philo/; accessed January 18, 2012.

6. René Descartes, *Discourse on Method*, 9.

7. Saint Augustine, *The Confessions of Saint Augustine* (a.d. 401), translated by Edward Bouverie Pusey; http://www.sacred-texts.com/chr/augconf.htm; accessed February 1, 2012.

8. John Calvin, *Institutes of the Christian Religion,* translated by Henry Beveridge (Grand Rapids, MI: William. B. Eerdmans, 2006).

9. Saint Augustine, *The Confessions of Saint Augustine* (a.d. 401), translated by Edward Bouverie Pusey; http://www.sacred-texts.com/chr/augconf.htm; accessed February 1, 2012.

10. Ralph McInerny and John O'Callaghan, "Aquinas' Moral, Political, and Legal Philosophy," *The Stanford Encyclopedia of Philosophy* (Fall 2011 edition), Edward N. Zalta (ed.); http://plato.stanford.edu/entries/aquinas-moral-political/; accessed February 1, 2012.

11. René Descartes, *Discourse on Method*.

12. Blaise Pascal, *Pensees* (London, England: Penguin Group), 128.

13. J. Gresham Machen, "God the Creator" *The Christian Faith in the Modern World*, (Grand Rapids MI: William. B. Eerdmans, 1993).

14. René Descartes, *Discourse on Method*.

15. Aristotle, *On The Soul*, cited in "Aristotle," *Internet Encyclopedia of Philosophy*; http://www.iep.utm.edu/aristotl/; accessed January 18, 2012.

## CHAPTER SEVEN

1. Myles Munroe, *Rediscovering The Kingdom* (Shippensburg, PA: Destiny Image, Publishers, Inc., 2004), 30.

2. Aristotle, *Physics Book III,* translated by David W. Graham (Clarendon Press, 1999).

3. Peter Hanns Refil and Ellen Judy Wilson, *Encyclopedia of the Enlightenment* (New York: Book Builders Inc. 1996), 443.

4. John Calvin, *Institutes of the Christian Religion*, translated by Henry Beveridge; http://www.ccel.org/ccel/calvin/institutes.toc.html; accessed January 18, 2012.

5. Saint Augustine, quoted on *ThinkExist.com;* http://thinkexist.com/quotation/faith_is_to_believe_what_you_do_not_see-the/219819.html; accessed February 1, 2012.

6. A.M. Hunter, *Interpreting Paul's Gospel* (London, England: SCM Press LTD, 1954).

## CHAPTER TEN

1. Cited in "Reasons for Faith," *A Catholic Response, Inc.;* http://users.binary.net/polycarp/reasons.html; accessed January 19, 2012.

2. Cited in "Reasons for Faith," *A Catholic Response, Inc.,* http://users.binary.net/polycarp/reasons.html; accessed January 19, 2012.

3. Blaise Pascal, *Pensees* (London, England: Penguin Group), 127.

4. Martin Luther, "The Large Catechism," translated by R. Bente and W.H.T. Dan; available at *Project Wittenberg;* http://www.iclnet.org/pub/resources/text/wittenberg/luther/catechism/web/cat-04.html; accessed January 19, 2012.

5. Blaise Pascal, *Pensees,* 121.

6. Albert Einstein, *The New Quotable Einstein*, ed. Alice Calaprice, (Princeton, NJ: Princeton University Press, 2005), 198.

7. *Ibid.,* 194.

8. *Ibid.,* 195.

9. Saint Augustine, *On the Morals of the Catholic Church;* available at http://www.newadvent.org/fathers/1401.htm; accessed February 1, 2012.

10. *Ibid.*

11. *Ibid.*

12. Paul Tillich, *A History of Christian Thought*, ed. Carle E. Braaten (New York: Simon and Schuster, 1968), 387.

## PART TWO WORD WEALTH

1. Kenneth S. Wuest, *Wuest's Word Studies in the Greek New Testament,* CD-ROM (Grand Rapids: William B. Eerdmans, 1997).

## PART TWO PRACTICAL APPLICATIONS

1. C.S. Lewis, "Is Theology Poetry?" *The Weight of Glory and other Addresses* (New York: Harper Collins, 1980), 140.

## CHAPTER ELEVEN

1. *Blue Letter Bible*, s.v. "Isopsychos" (Strong's Greek 2473); http://www.blueletterbible.org/lang/lexicon/Lexicon.cfm?strongs=G2473; and Bible Study Tools, s.v. "Homophron" (Strong's Greek 3675); http://www.biblestudytools.com/lexicons/greek/nas/homophron.html; accessed February 1, 2012.

2. Plato, *Laws: Book IV,* translated by Benjamin Jowett, available at *The Internet Classics Archive;* http://classics.mit.edu/Plato/laws.4.iv.html; accessed January 20, 2012.

3. John Calvin, "On the Christian Life," translated by Henry Bevridge, available at *Institute of the Christian Religion;* http://www.ccel.org/ccel/calvin/chr_life.html; accessed January 19, 2012.

4. John Locke, *An Essay Concerning the True Original Extent and End of Civil Government* (1690), available at http://www.pinkmonkey.com/dl/library1/book1283.pdf; accessed February 1, 2012.

5. Clement of Rome "An Exhortation to Humility" From the First Epistle of Clement to the Corinthians, prepared by Pontifical Theological Faculty (Rome, 2001), available at http://www.vatican.va/spirit/documents/spirit_20010627_clemente_en.html; accessed February 1, 2012.

## CHAPTER TWELVE

1. E.H. Gifford, quoted in Jeff Asher, "The Mind of Christ" *The Church of Christ in Zion, Illinois* (2011); http://www.padfield.com/2002/mind.html; accessed January 20, 2012.

2. Matthew Henry, *Matthew Henry's Commentary on the Whole Bible* (Bible Software by Johnhurt.com), Philippians 2:5-11.

3. "Hegel, George W. Friedrich," *Microsoft (R) Encarta.* (Microsoft Corporation; Funk & Wagnall's Corporation, 1993).

## CHAPTER FIFTEEN

1. Plato, *Laws: Book IV,* translated by Benjamin Jowett, available at *The Internet Classics Archive;* http://classics.mit.edu/Plato/laws.4.iv.html; accessed January 20, 2012.

2. John Calvin, *On the Christian Life*, translated by Henry Bevridge, *Institute of the Christian Religion* (public domain).

3. John Locke, *An Essay Concerning the True Original Extent and End of Civil Government* (1690), available at http://www.pinkmonkey.com/dl/library1/book1283.pdf; accessed February 1, 2012.

4. Saint Augustine, *The Confessions of Saint Augustine* (New York, NY: Bantam, 1960), 176.

5. Tom Bridges, "Aristotle: Lecture Notes 2," Philosophy and Religion Department; www.msu.org/ethics/contentethics/lecturenotes/aristotle/Aristotlelecture; accessed December 3, 2005.

6. Albert Einstein, *The New Quotable Einstein*, ed. Alice Calaprice, (Princeton, NJ: Princeton University Press, 2005), 195.

## PART THREE WORD WEALTH

1. W.E. Vine, *Vine's Complete Expository Dictionary of Old and New Testament Words* (Nashville, TN: Thomas Nelson, 1996), 251.

## CHAPTER SIXTEEN

1. Richard Baxter, quoted in John Piper, *Desiring God* (Multnomah, 1996), preface; http://www.desiringgod.org/dg/id86.htm; accessed February 2, 2012.

## CHAPTER SEVENTEEN

1. James Strong, *Strong's Exhaustive Concordance of the Bible* (Nashville, TN: Thomas Nelson, 1991), s.v. "Nous," Greek #3563.

2. Aristotle, *On The Soul*, cited in "Aristotle," *Internet Encyclopedia of Philosophy*; http://www.iep.utm.edu/aristotl/; accessed January 20, 2012.

## CHAPTER NINETEEN

1. C.H. Spurgeon, *Prayer Perfumed with Praise* (The Spurgeon Archive, April 1879); http://spurgeon.org/sermons/1469.htm; accessed January 20, 2012.

2. John MacArthur, *Christ Humbled/Christ Exalted, The Exaltation of Christ—Part 1* (San Diego, CA: Jesus Christ Saves Ministries, 2000); http://www.jcsm.org/StudyCenter/john_macarthur/50-17.htm; accessed February 1, 2012.

## CHAPTER TWENTY

1. Saint Thomas Aquinas, *Summa Theologica* (Benziger Bros., 1947); available at http://www.ccel.org/ccel/aquinas/summa; accessed January 20, 2012.

2. Aristotle, "Aristotle on Friendship," *Nicomachean Ethics Book 8*, Chaper 1.

3. Immanuel Kant, *The Critique of Practical Reason* (1788), translated by Thomas Kingsmill Abbott; http://philosophy.eserver.org/kant/critique-of-practical-reaso.txt; accessed February 1, 2012.

4. Charles Spurgeon *"Sermon Notes 242,"* available at http://www.scribd.com/doc/56969338/Charles-Spurgeon-Sermon-Notes-No-242; accessed February 1, 2012.

5. *Ibid.*

6. John Calvin, *On the Christian Life*, translated by Henry Bevridge, *Institute of the Christian Religion* (public domain).

7. Marcus Aurelius, quoted on *Brainy Quote*; http://www.brainyquote.com/quotes/quotes/m/marcusaure132163.html; accessed February 2, 2012.

8. Blaise Pascal, *Pensees* (London, England: Penguin Group), 224.

9. John Calvin, quoted on *BrainyQuote.com;* http://www.brainyquote.com/quotes/quotes/j/johncalvin182893.html; accessed January 20, 2012.

10. Martin Luther, quoted on *ThinkExist.com;* http://thinkexist.com/quotation/ no_man_ought_to_lay_a_cross_upon_himself-or_to/214900.html; accessed February 2, 2012.

11. C.S. Lewis, quoted in "Quotations by C.S. Lewis," Word Power; http:// wordpower.ws/quotations/c-s-lewis.html; accessed January 20, 2012.

# ABOUT NOEL JONES

Noel Jones has a reputation of being provocative and, some would say, controversial. But all would agree that he is among the great theologians of our time, and his skills in hermeneutics and homiletics are recognized and appreciated by many of his contemporaries. To say that he thinks and operates "out of the box" would be highly suggestive of his propensity to live life "on the edge." He challenges us to think on a higher plane, to go beyond the ordinary and normal when we study the Word of God, and seek to understand the mysteries of God. Bishop Jones does not want us to be religious or mystical, but to become practical students of the God of our salvation.

Jones is the third child of the late Bishop Robert Jones and Evangelist Marjorie Jones. He graduated from St. Jago High School in Spanish Town, Jamaica, and later attained a Bachelors degree in Theology from Aenon Bible College. He responded to his call to the ministry at the age of 19, accepted his first pastorate in Longview, Texas, at Bethel Temple of Longview at the age of 26, and later became the successor to the venerable Bishop Robert W. McMurray as shepherd to approximately 1,000 members of Greater Bethany Community Church in South Central Los Angeles, California. During his pastorate, the congregation has relocated to a sanctuary in Gardena, and the church, now called, The City of Refuge, accommodates a growing membership of over 17,000 members. Through the five services that are held there each week, the congregants are invigorated and transformed by the uniquely powerful preaching of this awesome man of God.

Bishop Jones is a scholar, an author, a philanthropist, a charismatic leader, and a powerful preacher. He is considered a "preaching machine," and is constantly sought out to express his views and share his methods of preparation and delivery of sermons. He is called upon nationally and internationally to minister to those lost and confused by a world that many times robs us of expectation and hope. His mantra for the 21st century has become that we must return to our first love, God. While we have been led to believe that our purpose in life is to seek health, wealth, and prosperity for the last 25 years, Jones feels that we have not encouraged people to come to know and understand the Word of God and His Lordship in our lives.

In Los Angeles, he hosts a weekly radio broadcast on Sunday nights on KJLH (AM Radio). Nationally he can be seen each week on the Word Network on Sunday afternoons.

His literary publications include *Battle for the Mind: How You Can Understand the Thoughts of God, God's Gonna Make You Laugh,* and *Vow of Prosperity.*

He is the father of three delightful children: Noel II (married to Cozzette), Tifani (married to Bavu), and Eric (married to Angela), and four grandchildren, Lena, Ian, Oliver, and Ellison.

# ABOUT REV. DR. GEORGIANNA A. LAND

Rev. Dr. Georgianna A. Land is an ordained minister in the AME Church and a retired college professor and educational administrator with a variety of experiences and achievements in educational, congressional, and governmental administration. She currently serves as a Foreign Affairs Officer at the Department of State in the office of the Special Representative for Global Intergovernmental Affairs, Office of the Secretary. Dr. Land is responsible for designing strategies for integrating domestic and foreign sub-national partnerships to improve local governance and public service delivery at the international, national, and local levels.

# IN THE RIGHT HANDS, THIS BOOK WILL CHANGE LIVES!

Most of the people who need this message will not be looking for this book. To change their lives, you need to put a copy of this book in their hands.

> *But others (seeds) fell into good ground, and brought forth fruit, some a hundred-fold, some sixty-fold, some thirty-fold* (Matthew 13:8).

Our ministry is constantly seeking methods to find the good ground, the people who need this anointed message to change their lives. Will you help us reach these people?

> *Remember this—a farmer who plants only a few seeds will get a small crop. But the one who plants generously will get a generous crop* (2 Corinthians 9:6).

## EXTEND THIS MINISTRY BY SOWING
### 3 BOOKS, 5 BOOKS, 10 BOOKS, OR MORE TODAY,
#### AND BECOME A LIFE CHANGER!

Thank you,

*Don Nori Sr.*

Don Nori Sr., Founder
Destiny Image
Since 1982